SALADS

SALADS

Fresh and favorite recipes for classic salads

Sue Mullin

CHARTWELL
BOOKS, INC.

A QUINTET BOOK

Published by Chartwell Books
A Division of Book Sales, Inc.
114 Northfield Avenue
Edison, New Jersey 08837

This edition produced for sale in the U.S.A., its
territories and dependencies only.

ISBN 0-7858-0554-0

This book was designed and produced by
Quintet Publishing Limited
6 Blundell Street
London N7 9BH

Creative Director: Richard Dewing
Designer: Peter Laws
Project Editor: Laura Sandelson
Photographer: David Armstrong
Home Economist: Gina Steer

Typeset in Great Britain by
Central Southern Typesetters, Eastbourne
Manufactured in Singapore by Eray Scan Pte Ltd.
Printed in Singapore by
Star Standard Industries (Pte) Ltd.

Contents

LEAVES, HERBS, AND OTHER SALAD INGREDIENTS

❖

I can remember when a salad meant little more than iceberg lettuce, onion, tomato, and – if the chef was really creative – some cucumbers and shredded carrots, usually dressed with oil and vinegar.

The number of foodstuffs stocked in the average supermarket produce section twenty years ago amounted to fewer than 65 items: today, more than 300 ingredients, many of them used in making salads, vie for space in overflowing bins. One of the reasons for this expansion is the relatively recent interest in olive oil. When the top-selling specialty food product at supermarkets became olive oils, it naturally followed that the produce section would blossom with a more international cornucopia of lettuces, herbs, vegetables, and fruits. Today, there are so many leaves, sprigs, herbs, and other salad ingredients in most supermarkets – not to mention gourmet and ethnic food stores – that some days I feel like toting a botanical guide with me when I go shopping.

We can all rejoice that the crunchy ingredients going into salads are not just trendy; they are also good for our health. Gone are the days when gourmet cooking meant throwing a pint of cream and a bottle of brandy into a stew. We have entered the day of the "designer greens," as some food writers have called arugula, radicchio, and the ever-growing list of salad items; many of which were eaten by ancient Romans and Greeks, but are only now becoming widely popular. And if we want to stay on top of the trend, we need to know our arugula from our zucchini, and that radicchio is pronounced *radikio*, not *radicchio*.

Lots of other ingredients are used in salads in addition to greens such as vegetables, fruits, nuts, onions, and cheeses, to name but a few and if the ingredient is unusual, I will say a word about it with the recipe.

COMBINING SALAD GREENS

In general, the darker the green, the stronger the flavor. If you are using a mild-flavored lettuce, such as iceberg, you may want to add peppery notes by combining it with watercress, arugula, young dandelion, or nasturtium blossoms. Conversely, you would probably not want to mix a salad with too many strong flavors. New York food writer Mindy Heiferling calls salads, such as Arugula, Radicchio and Chicory Frisée with Duck Cracklings and Warm Sorrel Vinaigrette, which she found on a restaurant menu, "Nouvelle Hell." I strongly agree. Nibble and nosh as you toss. Your tastebuds are, ultimately, your best guide.

PREPARING AND STORING SALAD GREENS

Firm lettuces are easily cleaned by cutting out the stem. Sever it about an inch deep into the head, and hold the lettuce under running cold water. Then turn the head right-side up on a colander placed in the sink. Remove the outside wilted leaves, pull the head apart, pat the leaves dry with a clean dishcloth or paper towel, and put the lettuce in the refrigerator to crisp. Romaine, escarole, and other clusters of firm lettuce leaves may be pulled apart first, then washed, patted dry, and crisped in the refrigerator. Use a little more care with Boston, field, and other

soft lettuces. Float the leaves in cold water and spread them out on paper towels to air-dry.

Remove large, gritty, tough stems from spinach by folding the leaves in half lengthwise so that the sides touch, then pull the stems down along the leaves.

To store greens, line a perforated, thick, plastic bag with slightly damp paper towels, insert the greens, and refrigerate. Chill your salad plates, too, if you want to really show off your icy greens. If you want to hurry things up, or you have a difficult time keeping greens fresh for several days, try some of the already washed and bagged greens at your grocer's. They are more expensive, but at least you won't end up discarding them. Some come with packets of dressings, too, but they are usually full of preservatives and calories, and you will probably want to replace them with your own homemade varieties.

PREPARING AND STORING HERBS

Rinse herbs in cold water and remove discolored leaves before using. Fresh herbs are bursting with flavor and only a single strong pungent herb is used in many salads so that one flavor doesn't cancel out another. To keep herbs from turning an unsightly brown, place them in an airtight glass jar or plastic container and refrigerate. If your herbs have their stems attached, such as parsley or cilantro, store in the refrigerator in a lidded glass or in a jar with water covering the roots.

You can freeze any leftover small bunches of green herbs, such as mint or chives, by washing and drying them, wrapping them in aluminum foil or plastic, and placing them in the freezer where they will stay flavorful for about two months. Use these frozen herbs for cooking only, though, because while freezing doesn't ruin the flavor, it does make them look limp.

Dried herbs are used directly from their containers. Because they are stronger than fresh herbs, so substitute a teaspoon of dried herb for a tablespoon of fresh. Store dried herbs away from heat in a cool, dimly lit place. They will keep for up to a year.

DRYING HERBS

You can dry your own by tying stems of herbs together in small bunches and hanging them upside down and out of direct sunlight in a closet, attic, or kitchen. When herbs are dry, in about two weeks' time, place them on a paper towel and rub the stems between your palms until all the leaves have fallen off. For thyme, rosemary, and oregano, you can strip the leaves from the stem by simply running your thumb and index finger down the stem. Discard the stems and then rub leaves through a fine-mesh strainer to remove any small bits of stray stem. Store your dried leaves in a glass jar with a tight-fitting lid, and label the jars carefully.

Glossary of Salad Greens

Chervil

Chives

ARUGULA

This green herb is also called rocket, roquette, rucola, and ruchetta. It has a soft texture and peppery, sharp taste. Many cooks believe it is best used alone in salads, served with only a simple dressing.

BASIL

This sweet, perfumey "royal herb" of ancient Greece is a member of the mint family and has a flavor like licorice and cloves. It is a staple in Mediterranean cooking. Fresh basil makes a beautiful garnish, but you can also buy it dried.

BIBB

Before the new designer greens became popular, yellowy green bibb, grown in limestone soil, was the most sought-after lettuce. It has a tender texture and sharp flavor, which goes well with rich dressings and ingredients, such as crab. It is also good when mixed with other greens.

Basil

BOK CHOY

Sometimes called *pak choi*, Chinese chard, or white mustard cabbage, this elongated cabbage unfurls dark green leaves from long white stalks. *Choi* can be translated as both cabbage and the generic term for vegetable, and the green is beloved by the Chinese. Choose heads with smooth white stalks and crisp, unblemished leaves. It will keep for about four days if stored in a plastic bag in the refrigerator.

BOSTON

This lettuce is also called butter, Simpson, and, incorrectly, bibb. It is a round, loosely packed head with tender, soft leaves and a mild flavor.

BRONZE

Also called red lettuce, this garden lettuce has bronze-edged leaves and is similar in texture and taste to leaf (or garden) lettuce.

BUTTERHEAD

There are several varieties of this type of lettuce, which is soft, crisp, and similar to bibb. It is folded into loose rosettes and the outer leaves on some varieties are a pretty red-wine color.

CABBAGE

A firmly packed head of thick, heavy, pale green or purple-red leaves. Discard the tough outer leaves before using. Cabbage is usually shredded and used in coleslaw or mixed with salad greens.

CHERVIL

A fern-like plant with feathery anise-flavored leaves, chervil is used in salads and cold dishes. It is one of the classic ingredients in *fines herbes*.

Dill

Belgian Endive

CHICORY

Called frisée by the French, and curly endive by some English speakers, this green has feathery but sturdy leaves that spread out. Chicory is yellow at the center, and becomes a pale to darker green outside. Its crisp texture and slightly bitter taste adds pizzazz to a mix of other, more delicately flavored, greens.

CHIVES

This long, thin onion grass has a pleasing, subtle, mild flavor that seems to spread over the palate. The blossoms can also be eaten.

CILANTRO

Also known as fresh coriander, culantro, or Chinese parsley, this herb has a pungent mintiness and is related to the parsley family. Some think it tastes like citrus zest, while others find its flavor soapy, so use the herb judiciously if company is expected. It is used in the cuisines of Mexico, the Orient, the Caribbean, and India.

Cilantro

CORN SALAD

Also called mâche and lamb's lettuce, this delicate but full-flavored European lettuce has downy, medium-to-dark, blue-green, spoon-shaped leaves and a sweet, nutty flavor. It is excellent when dressed with a classic vinaigrette.

DANDELION

Long considered an ugly, invasive weed in the United States, dandelion leaves are cultivated in France, and dandelion-growers are beginning to appear in the States. The tart flavor of the narrow, spiky, dark green leaves seems to be appealing to more and more people.

Chicory

DILL

This herb has a light caraway flavor and feathery, fern-like green leaves. Traditionally, it is used in making pickles, for flavoring Indian yogurt dishes and in gravlax, but it is now being used in salads, too. The herb makes a lovely garnish, especially for fish dishes.

ENDIVE

Also called Belgian endive, this green grows on a firm, narrow, pale yellow head and has tightly packed, long, pointed, waxy leaves and a tangy flavor. Its leaves can transform a salad into a still-life masterpiece.

ESCAROLE

Also known as batavian endive, batavia, or chicory escarole, this somewhat bitter lettuce has a flat spread-out head with a yellow center. The dark green leaves are curly, firm, and robust in texture.

FIELD LETTUCE

Also called lamb's tongue, this lettuce has very small spears on delicate stems and a mild flavor.

ICEBERG

A round, firm lettuce, this longtime American favorite keeps well and is crispy, but it is watery and not very flavorful. It does, however, deliver the requisite crunch that many people demand in a salad or a sandwich.

LEAF LETTUCE

Also called garden lettuce, there are several varieties of this pleasant, mild-tasting lettuce with soft, long, crumpled-edged leaves. It is often used to prettify a delicate salad or to embellish and add crunch to hearty submarine sandwiches.

MESCLUN

This term, popular on restaurant menus, simply means "mixture" in French. It is usually a combination of lettuces, chicories, arugula, or watercress, and other herb greens. Because some of the leaves are smaller than more standard lettuce leaves, such as iceberg, mesclun is sometimes called "baby greens."

Scallions

Oak Leaf

MINT

This herb is available in many varieties, including apple mint, spearmint, and peppermint. It makes a lovely decoration and flavor enhancer for desserts and fruit salads.

MISTICANZA

Like the French word "mesclun," this is simply a mixture of lettuces.

MUSTARD GREENS

These bright, light green leaves have scalloped edges and a soft texture. They have a pungent mustard flavor that is delicious with robust foods, such as beef.

NASTURTIUM

The flower heads of nasturtium add a peppery taste and gorgeous color to a green or mixed salad. Use only fresh, unsprayed blossoms.

OAK LEAF

Also called salad bowl, red oak leaf, and lolla rossa, this tangy lettuce is available in both red and green colors. Its velvety leaves are paddle-shaped, like oak leaves, and it makes a pretty addition to any salad.

PARSLEY

Varieties include the familiar curly-leaf and the increasingly popular Italian flat-leaf. The herb looks pretty, tastes clean, and refreshes the breath. It's also rich in vitamins. Use the fresh herb; dried parsley is tasteless.

PINE NUTS

These are actually the kernels of the pine-tree seed. They are tender and cream-colored with a slightly oily, delicate flavor. These were a native staple crop of the Pueblo Indians. These nuts are often toasted when used in salads.

Mint

Flat leaf Parsley

Radicchio

RADICCHIO

Also called red chicory, this crisp, trendy, slightly bitter lettuce is as Italian as its name. Its small leaves are a colorful addition to other greens in a mixed salad and can also be used as a capacious "cup" for salads, particularly seafood salads.

ROMAINE

Also called Cos or Kos (the name comes from the Greek island of Kos), this lettuce has an elongated, cylindrical head and long, stiff, thick-veined leaves, which are usually medium-dark to dark green on the outside and greenish-white or pale yellow near the center. Unlike most lettuces, the lighter-colored leaves have the stronger flavor. It is pungent and hardy, chock-full of vitamins and minerals, and good with assertive dishes, such as Caesar salad.

SCALLIONS

Often called green onions, scallions have long, thin stems with white bulbs and green tops. They can often be substituted for chives.

SHALLOTS

This member of the onion family, originating in the Middle East, has a small, round, pinkish-white bulb and golden brown skin. It has a subtle, complex flavor that's somewhere between onions and garlic. The great chefs adore shallots, which are now being used in elegant Oriental dishes, as well as in French cuisine.

SPINACH

This herb was first grown in Persia and the Middle East. It has dark green leaves, some crinkly, on stems. After lettuce, spinach is the most popular green leaf in North America, although most of it is consumed in cooked form. Some find raw spinach hard to digest, so use it judiciously in salads prepared for guests.

Spinach

Tarragon

TARRAGON

This is a tall plant that tastes like peppery anise. It is used in classic French cooking and makes a great flavoring for vinegar.

TURNIP GREENS

These can resemble napped radish leaves and have a sharp taste. Remove large stems by folding leaves in half lengthwise, then pull the stems down along the leaves. The bulb can be shredded and eaten raw.

WATERCRESS

This green grows on small stalks and has many small, round, dark green petals. Watercress is sold banded in bunches and has a distinct, lively, pleasant taste.

Watercress

OILS AND VINEGARS

❖

Oils and vinegars are the basic ingredients that liven up salad greens. Combining two parts of oil and one part vinegar, then adding a little sugar, salt, or pepper to taste, makes a tasty coating for greens. Adjust the ratio of oil and vinegar according to the acidity of the vinegar you use, the type of oil, and your own tastebuds.

If you like tomato in your salads, but are subject to heartburn, it is wise to place the tomatoes on top of the salad after tossing. Tomatoes have a lot of acid, and there is even more acid in vinegar. Japanese rice vinegar is less acidic, and you may want to use it instead of the more standard vinegars.

If you are concerned about cholesterol – and oils are loaded with fats, some good and some bad – try using less than a half-and-half ratio, or substitute a little extracted fresh vegetable juice for some of the oil in a recipe. If you like creamy dressings, but want to avoid dairy fat, add about a tablespoon each of milk and Dijon mustard to an 8-ounce carton of plain low-fat or non-fat yogurt, then season the mixture with a teaspoon of dried herbs, or one or two teaspoons of fresh herbs, and a dab of honey.

Oil and vinegars can be stored in attractive bottles to display in the kitchen or pantry. Imagine how pretty they will be if stored in beautiful Spanish green glass bottles, glass Granada-style bottles, or any pretty wine bottles you have saved. A fish-shaped wine bottle and round-sided, clear, slivovitz bottle are my favorites. Just remember to tightly cork or seal the bottles.

OILS FOR SALADS

Do not store any oils near the stove, or any other warm area, because heat can cause deterioration. Refrigeration, on the other hand, can make oils turn milky-looking and cause them to congeal. Simply place them on a shelf in a cupboard or on display but out of sunlight. Most oils generally have plenty of vitamin E in them, a substance that keeps them from turning rancid quickly, but polyunsaturated oils turn rancid rapidly unless treated with preservatives and should be refrigerated. Olive oil keeps for about a year in the refrigerator, but it will congeal and turn cloudy, so return it to room temperature before using. It can be stored on the shelf for up to six months. Delicate oils, such as walnut or infused olive oils, should be refrigerated and used rapidly.

INFUSED OILS

These are oils that have herbs steeped or soaked in them. They have long been used in Mediterranean, Indian, Chinese, and other Asian cooking. It is best to buy infused oils that have been commercially prepared because preparing infused oils at home, especially those oils containing garlic and onion, can cause botulism. Commercially prepared and with the proper preservatives, however, these oils can be considered perfectly safe – and delicious. They should be refrigerated after opening.

A store-bought infused oil can liven up a vinaigrette. Or you can dip dense bread into flavored oil for an imaginative alternative to butter. Flavored oil can also provide the perfect complement to pasta, pizza, or bruschetta. Infused oil can top a baked potato or substitute for butter and milk to make garlicky mashed potatoes. You could also try sautéeing fresh artichoke hearts in an infused oil, or drizzling a little over poached salmon, broiled eggplant, roasted peppers, or other vegetables. A low-fat or non-fat prepared mayonnaise can also be jazzed up with a little infused oil.

Glossary of Salad Oils

CANOLA OIL OR RAPESEED OIL
This oil contains one-twelfth of the saturated fat contained in tropical oils, such as coconut oil.

CORN OIL
This oil is also low in saturated fat. Although rather bland, it can be used for frying and baking, as well as in salad dressings.

HAZELNUT OIL
Extracted from hazelnuts, this oil is very aromatic. It can be combined with a less strongly flavored oil for a rich, nutty-tasting salad dressing. Heat destroys its flavor.

OLIVE OIL
A staple in the Mediterranean diet, olive oil is healthy, as well as tasty. It is the best oil to use in a simple dressing such as a vinaigrette or as a velvety "thickener" in many other dressings.

PEANUT OIL
Extracted from peanuts, this oil is often used in Asian dishes, but can also be used in many salad dressings. It is slightly higher in saturated fat than canola and corn oil.

SAFFLOWER OIL
This, a delicate, relatively tasteless oil is low in saturated fat.

SESAME OIL
Extracted from sesame seeds, this oil is used in Chinese cooking. Like peanut oil, it is slightly higher in saturated fat than canola and corn oil, but not nearly as fatty as tropical oils.

TROPICAL OILS
These oils – such as coconut, palm, or palm kernel – are highly saturated and should be avoided if possible.

WALNUT OIL
Extracted from walnuts, this oil is used in well-known salads, such as the Waldorf. It has a rich flavor, which is destroyed by heating it, and should be used sparingly.

VINEGARS AND OTHER ACIDIC FLAVORINGS

Vinegar, a major food preservative and pickler, is as old as civilization itself. In 400 B.C., Hippocrates used it to treat patients, and people still use it today for everything from headaches to removing lime deposits on fine crystal. Vinegar contains essential amino acids, vitamins, minerals, and enzymes. It is receptive to added flavors and keeps indefinitely in a cool, dark place. Furthermore, it is perfectly safe to make and keep preserved vinegars at home.

Most herbs can be used to flavor vinegars, tarragon, rosemary, thyme, marjoram, parsley, basil, fennel, dill, and sage. They can be used individually or in combinations. It's best to use fresh herbs; if you pick them yourself, make sure to select sprigs without any flowers. Bruising the herbs slightly will help to release their flavor. Try placing a little fresh oregano and small fresh chiles in a clean, dry bottle filled with white or red wine vinegar. Leave the vinegar for 2–3 weeks to infuse; try to make a point of shaking it every day. Strain the vinegar, pressing down well on the herbs. Taste to see if the herb flavor is strong enough. If it is not, repeat the process. Then use the finished vinegar to make a spicy salad dressing. Experiment with other fresh herbs, and store your creations in pretty bottles. You will have made a vinegar for pennies that specialty stores sell at prices approaching good table wine.

It is also possible to flavor vinegar with fruit for a fresh dressing for rich meats such as duck or game and a perfect complement to salads containing fruit. Try a raspberry vinegar mixed with walnut oil, mustard, salt, and pepper for an unforgettable vinaigrette.

Because vinegar and vinaigrettes have such powerful flavorings, it is important to consider when to serve them in the course of a meal. The French have the right idea on salads containing vinegar. They serve them after the main course so that the vinegar does not interfere with the wine. Wine or no wine, Americans prefer their salads with vinaigrettes at the start of a meal. If you are watching your weight, you might want to consider eating a large salad of mixed greens and raw vegetables sprinkled with a vinaigrette. Vinegar is known to suppress the appetite in some people, and might enable you to cut down on your main course and dessert portions.

There are many vinegars readily available today from supermarkets and specialty stores. Balsamic vinegar is a barrel-aged vinegar, dark in color with a mellow sweet-sour character. It is made from the Trebbiano grape in the region surrounding Modena, Italy, and aged in wooden casks for between two and forty years. Drizzle some on fish for a change from lemon, or use in marinades and dressings.

————— Glossary of Salad Vinegars —————

CHAMPAGNE VINEGAR
This vinegar is flavored with champagne.

CIDER VINEGAR
Made from the juice of apples, this vinegar has a fruity flavor that works well in salads. It is also used for pickling and preserving.

DISTILLED WHITE VINEGAR
Made from grain alcohol, this vinegar is used mostly in pickling. It has a harsh flavor.

MALT VINEGAR
Made from barley, this vinegar is mostly used for pickling but can also be used in salad dressings.

RASPBERRY VINEGAR
Made from raspberries and vinegar, this vinegar has a fruity flavor that is good in fruit salads.

RICE WINE VINEGAR
Made from sake, this vinegar has a natural sweetness and is used predominantly in Chinese and Japanese cooking.

SHERRY VINEGAR
Made from Spanish sherry, this vinegar is aged and has a subtle sweetness from the brandy that is used in sherry-making. It makes a wonderful ingredient in salad dressings.

WINE VINEGARS
Either red or white, these vinegars are excellent in dressings and are very versatile. White wine vinegar is a good choice for an infused vinegar.

Garlic Vinegar

Makes about 3 cups

INGREDIENTS

12 plump garlic cloves
3 cups white wine vinegar
garlic cloves for garnish, optional

❖ Lightly crush the garlic cloves and put them into a jar or bottle. Pour in the vinegar, cover, and shake the jar or bottle. Leave in a cool, dark place for 2–3 weeks.

❖ If the flavor of the vinegar is strong enough, strain it and re-bottle. If desired, thread 2–3 garlic cloves per bottle onto a wooden cocktail stick and add to the bottles.

Vinegar Flavored with Herbes de Provence

Makes about 3 cups

INGREDIENTS

3 large sprigs of tarragon
3 large sprigs of thyme
3 sprigs of rosemary
4 bay leaves
pinch of fennel seeds
3 cups white wine vinegar

❖ Lightly bruise the herbs and then pack them into a jar or bottle. Pour in the vinegar and close the bottle tightly. Shake the jar or bottle and leave in a cool, dark place for 2–3 weeks, shaking the jar or bottle daily.

❖ Strain the vinegar, pressing down well on the herbs. Taste the vinegar to see if the herb flavor is strong enough. If it is not, repeat the process. A fresh herb sprig can be added to the prepared vinegar, if desired.

Fruit Vinegars

Makes about 2 cups

INGREDIENTS

*1 lb. fruit, such as raspberries,
strawberries, or blackcurrants
2 cups white wine vinegar
2 tbsp. sugar*

❖ Put the fruit into a non-reactive bowl or jar. Add a little of the vinegar and crush the fruit with the back of a wooden spoon to release the juice. Add the remaining vinegar, cover, and leave in a cool place for 1 week, stirring occasionally.

❖ Strain the vinegar into a saucepan, add the sugar and heat gently until the sugar has dissolved. Bring to the boil; let cool.

❖ Pour the vinegar into a clean bottle, cover and store in a dark, cool place.

Orange Vinegar

Makes about 4 cups

INGREDIENTS

*3 large oranges
4 cups white wine vinegar
1 small orange, for garnish*

❖ Pare the rind from the 3 large oranges, taking care not to include any white pith. Put the rind into a clean large jar. Cut the 3 oranges in half and squeeze out the juice. Pour into the jar, seal, and shake. Leave in a cool, dark place for 3 weeks, shaking the jar occasionally.

❖ Strain the vinegar and re-bottle. Thinly pare some of the rind from the small orange so no pith is included. Cut the rind into thin strips and add 3 strips to each bottle.

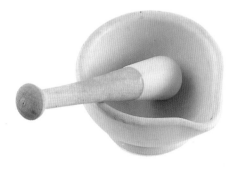

Section One

SALAD DRESSINGS
AND VINAIGRETTES

Florida Vinaigrette

Makes about 2 cups

INGREDIENTS

1 cup fresh or bottled lime or lemon juice
¼ cup finely chopped onion
1 red bell pepper, cored, seeded, and finely chopped
1 tbsp. finely chopped ginger root
1 tbsp. minced garlic
2 tbsp. finely chopped fresh dill
1 tbsp. Dijon-style mustard
1 tsp. rice wine vinegar
½ cup light olive oil or ½ cup of the juice extracted from red bell peppers with 2 tsp. olive oil added
salt and freshly ground black pepper

In Florida, the juice of freshly squeezed Key limes would be used for this tart vinaigrette, but even made with bottled citrus juice this dressing tastes great. Drizzle the vinaigrette over salad greens, or douse over poached and chilled seafood, such as shrimp or scallops: it also adds pizzazz to roasted potatoes and steamed vegetables.

———————— ❖ ————————

❖ Whisk together the lime or lemon juice, onion, pepper, ginger, garlic, dill, mustard, vinegar, and olive oil or red bell pepper juice in a nonreactive medium-size bowl until well combined. Season with salt and pepper to taste.

Continental Herb Dressing

Makes about 1 cup

INGREDIENTS

½ cup vegetable oil
¼ cup vinegar
¼ tsp. salt
dash of cayenne pepper
1 tbsp. finely chopped fresh parsley
1 tbsp. finely chopped fresh basil
1 tbsp. finely chopped fresh chervil
1 tbsp. finely chopped fresh oregano
freshly ground black pepper

You can almost see spring making its long-awaited debut after a cold winter in this aromatic dressing, which incorporates favorite European herbs. It is delicious served over any mixture of greens, particularly French Mesclun (see page 48).

———————— ❖ ————————

❖ Whisk together the vegetable oil, vinegar, salt, cayenne pepper, and herbs in a medium-size bowl. Add pepper to taste and chill in the refrigerator for 2–24 hours.

RIGHT *Florida Vinaigrette*

Classic French Vinaigrette

Makes about 1 cup

INGREDIENTS
½ tsp. salt
⅛ tsp. freshly ground pepper
¼ cup vinegar or lemon juice
¼–½ tsp. Dijon-style mustard
¾ cup walnut or olive oil

In the United States, this vinaigrette was the first recipe listed under salad dressings in the 1896 *Boston Cooking-School Cook Book*, one of the first definitive cookbooks published in the country. This recipe includes prepared mustard, a fairly modern addition to the blend.

❖

❖ Whisk together the salt, pepper, vinegar or lemon juice, mustard, and walnut or olive oil in a nonreactive medium-size bowl until well combined. The dressing will keep for about 3 days in the refrigerator.

Emigré's Cooked French Dressing

Makes about 1 cup

INGREDIENTS
½ tbsp. salt
½ tbsp. dry mustard
1¼ tbsp. sugar
1 egg, lightly beaten
2½ tbsp. melted unsalted butter
¾ cup cream
dash of cayenne pepper
¼ cup white wine vinegar

A nobleman who emigrated from France, Chevalier d'Albignac, is said to have introduced salads of raw greens dressed in vinaigrettes to England in the late 1700s. While his recipes have been lost to history, they were reportedly just as complex as this one, which I have named after him. It tastes great over any mixture of salad greens.

❖

❖ Mix salt, mustard, sugar, egg, melted butter, cream, and cayenne pepper together in a nonreactive bowl. Add vinegar a teaspoon at a time, whisking constantly. Transfer to a double boiler and cook over boiling water, stirring constantly until the mixture thickens. Let cool and serve.

RIGHT *The ingredients for Classic French Vinaigrette*

Confetti Ranch Dressing

Confetti Ranch Dressing

Makes about 1 ¼ cups

INGREDIENTS
1 large garlic clove, ground into a paste
with a knife, mortar and pestle, or
garlic press
2 tbsp. olive oil
1 cup yogurt
1 red bell pepper, finely chopped
1 green bell pepper, finely chopped
1 yellow bell pepper, finely chopped
½ tsp. cumin
¼ tsp. dried cayenne or Tabasco
½ tsp. finely chopped fresh cilantro
(optional)
salt and freshly ground black pepper

This topping is a cool, refreshing treat when poured over crunchy salad greens or drizzled on melon or a combination of shredded raw turnips and red grapes. Use low-fat or non-fat yogurt to cut calories, if desired.

❖

❖ Place the garlic, olive oil, yogurt, bell peppers, cumin, cayenne or Tabasco, and cilantro in a medium-size bowl and mix together to combine. Season with salt and pepper to taste. Chill in the refrigerator for 2–24 hours. The dressing will keep in the refrigerator for about 3 days.

Mint-Ricotta Smoothie Dressing

Makes about 1 ½ cups

INGREDIENTS
1⅓ cups light or part-skim ricotta cheese
4 tbsp. finely chopped fresh mint
4–6 tbsp. freshly squeezed or bottled
lime juice
3 tsp. superfine sugar

This creamy blend is wonderful on fresh fruit, particularly melons, berries, peaches, apples, or pears. Ricotta is creamy without being high in dairy fat, so enjoy this topping without fretting about pounds.

❖

❖ Place the ricotta cheese in a food processor or blender, and purée for 2 minutes until smooth. Transfer to a bowl. Stir in the mint, lime juice, and sugar. The dressing will keep for about 3 days in the refrigerator.

Orange-Poppy Seed Dressing

Makes about ½ cup

INGREDIENTS

½ cup plain or vanilla low-fat yogurt
½ tbsp. honey
½ tsp. dry mustard
1 tbsp. grated onion
½ tbsp. frozen orange juice concentrate, thawed
½ tsp. poppy seeds
2 drops Tabasco or other hot pepper sauce (optional)
½ tsp. finely grated orange or lemon peel

This dressing originates from Pennsylvania-Dutch country, around Lancaster, Pennsylvania, and various farming regions of the Midwest. It combines well with fruit and avocado salads.

———— ❖ ————

In a medium bowl, place the yogurt, honey, dry mustard, onion, orange juice concentrate, poppy seeds, Tabasco, and orange or lemon peel in a medium-size bowl and stir well to combine. Cover and chill in the refrigerator for 2–24 hours. The dressing will keep about 3 days in the refrigerator.

Nutty Oriental Dressing

Makes about 1¼ cups

INGREDIENTS

1½ tbsp. peanut, sesame, or canola oil
1 garlic clove, chopped
1 tbsp. oyster sauce
1 tbsp. nuoc nam fish sauce or Thai nam pla fish sauce
pinch of sugar
1 tbsp. finely chopped fresh or canned chile pepper
5 tbsp. fresh mint leaves, sliced if large
5 tbsp. crushed dry-roasted peanuts

Inspired by Vietnamese cooking, this tasty dressing is great on lamb and other hot or cold meats, as well as on salad greens. If you like assertive flavors, you can also pour a little over rice noodles. You can find *nuoc nam* fish sauce at Asian markets.

———— ❖ ————

❖ Warm the oil in a wok, but do not let it sizzle. Add the garlic, oyster sauce, fish sauce, sugar, and chile, stirring constantly. Stir in the mint, remove from the heat, and let cool to room temperature. Add the peanuts and serve immediately.

RIGHT *Orange and Poppy Seed Dressing with avocados*

Dill Dressing

Makes about 2 cups

INGREDIENTS

1 cup plain non-fat or low-fat yogurt
1 cup prepared non-fat or low-fat
mayonnaise
1 tbsp. chopped scallions
1½ tbsp. finely chopped fresh dill
2 tsp. lemon juice
freshly ground black pepper

This is a perfect dressing for a cucumber salad, but it also makes a great dip for crudités, or serve it with fish for a refreshing change from tartar sauce. It can also be used instead of plain mayonnaise to make deviled eggs.

❖ Place the yogurt, mayonnaise, scallion, dill, and lemon juice in a medium-size bowl and mix together well to combine. Season with pepper to taste. Cover and chill in the refrigerator for 2–24 hours. Serve chilled.

Russian Doll Dressing

Makes about 1½ cups

INGREDIENTS

1 cup light or non-fat mayonnaise
1 tbsp. prepared horseradish, or grated
fresh horseradish
3 tbsp. chilled caviar or salmon roe
1 tsp. Worcestershire sauce
¼ tsp. Tabasco or other hot pepper sauce
1 tsp. grated onion

If you like caviar, you will love this Russian dressing. Use it to toss with salad greens or potatoes, or spoon it over a combination of diced potatoes and beets. It makes an elegant topping for potato pancakes.

❖ Place the mayonnaise, horseradish, caviar or salmon roe, Worcestershire sauce, Tabasco, and onion in a small bowl and mix well to combine. Serve immediately.

Homemade Mayonnaise

Makes about ¾ cup

INGREDIENTS

1 egg, or equivalent ⅛ cup egg product
1 tsp. dry mustard
dash of cayenne pepper
1 tsp. sugar
½ cup olive or vegetable oil
3 tbsp. lemon juice
salt

Emulsifying this versatile dressing by hand can take patience and a strong wrist, but a tasty version can be made quickly in a food processor or blender. If you substitute pasteurized egg product for the whole egg and use light olive or vegetable oil, you can reduce cholesterol, fat, and calories, in addition to eliminating any concerns about the safety of using raw eggs.

❖

❖ In a food processor or blender, combine the egg or egg product, dry mustard, cayenne pepper, sugar, and ¼ cup of the oil. Process on a high speed for 1 minute. Add the lemon juice and blend on high again for 10 seconds. Turn the food processor or blender to low, and add the remaining oil, a little at a time, until thick. Add salt to taste, and serve or store in the refrigerator.

Low-fat Blue Cheese Dressing

Makes about 1½–2 cups

INGREDIENTS

1 cup plain non-fat or low-fat yogurt
4 oz. blue cheese, crumbled
½ cup buttermilk
¼ cup finely chopped fresh parsley
1 tbsp. light olive oil
1 tsp. dry sherry or cider vinegar
freshly ground black pepper

This dressing is delicious served over salad greens. Although it tastes creamy and rich, it is low in fat because yogurt and buttermilk replace the traditional oil or mayonnaise.

❖

❖ Place the yogurt, cheese, buttermilk, parsley, olive oil, and sherry or vinegar in a small bowl and mix together to combine. Season with pepper to taste. Cover and chill for 2–24 hours before using. The dressing will keep for about 3 days in the refrigerator.

Try My Thai Dressing

Makes about 1 cup

INGREDIENTS

2 shallots, finely chopped
2 garlic cloves, finely chopped
2 tbsp. finely chopped fresh cilantro
½–1 tsp. crushed dried red pepper flakes
¼ cup Thai nam pla *fish sauce or*
Vietnamese nuoc nam *fish sauce*
¼ cup fresh lemon or lime juice
1 tsp. finely grated lemon or lime peel
3 scallions, finely chopped

This Thai-inspired dressing is especially good with steamed or broiled eggplant, which has been cooled to room temperature. It is also delicious when served over salad greens that have some julienned purple cabbage mixed in for color and texture.

❖

❖ Place the shallots, garlic, cilantro, red pepper flakes, fish sauce, lemon or lime juice, lemon or lime peel, and scallions in a nonreactive bowl and mix well to combine. Set aside at room temperature for about 15 minutes to let the flavors blend, then serve.

Green Goddess Dressing

Makes about 2 cups

INGREDIENTS

1 cup Homemade Mayonnaise (see
page 29), or a commercial variety
1 garlic clove, finely chopped.
3 anchovy fillets, drained on paper towels
and finely chopped
¼ cup snipped chives or finely chopped
scallion
¼ cup finely chopped fresh parsley
1 tbsp. lemon juice
1 tbsp. tarragon vinegar
½ cup sour cream

Created in San Francisco, this dressing is named for a popular 1930 movie. Anchovy gives the dressing its kick, while the chives or scallions and parsley impart the lovely green color. Serve on any combination of salad greens, or tossed with pasta or potatoes. You may like to use low-fat or non-fat mayonnaise and sour cream to reduce fat and calories.

❖

❖ Whisk together the mayonnaise, garlic, anchovy, chives or scallions, parsley, lemon juice, vinegar, and sour cream in a medium-size bowl to combine well. The dressing will keep for about 3 days in the refrigerator.

RIGHT *Try My Thai Dressing with steamed eggplant*

Dreamy California Dressing drizzled over mixed greens

Dreamy California Vinaigrette

Makes about ¾ cup

INGREDIENTS

2 tbsp. chopped fresh cilantro
1 tbsp. minced garlic
¼ cup balsamic vinegar
2 tbsp. sugar
½ cup olive oil or light olive oil
salt and freshly ground black pepper

This light dressing partners well with beefsteak tomatoes and most types of salad greens and mushrooms – the fancier the better. Top your salads with this vinaigrette and lots of goat cheese for a California touch.

——————— ❖ ———————

❖ In a nonreactive bowl, whisk together the cilantro, garlic, vinegar, sugar, and oil. Season with salt and pepper to taste. The dressing will keep for about 3 days in the refrigerator.

Citrusy French Dressing

Makes about ¾ cup

INGREDIENTS

3 tbsp. fresh or bottled lemon or lime juice
½ tsp. salt
⅛ tsp. black pepper
¼ tsp. sugar
¼ tsp. dry mustard (optional)
½ cup olive, sesame, or canola oil

This recipe makes a refreshing dressing for all sorts of seafood salads, such as shrimp, lobster, squid, and tuna.

——————— ❖ ———————

❖ Place the lemon or lime juice, salt, pepper, sugar, and dry mustard in a food processor or blender and blend on high until mixed. Add the oil a teaspoon at a time until well combined.

❖ Alternatively, whisk all the ingredients, except the oil, in a small bowl, then add the oil a little at a time, whisking continuously until the oil is incorporated.

Cal-Ital Sun-dried Tomato Dressing

Makes about 1½ cups

INGREDIENTS

*12 sun-dried tomatoes, soaked in water
until plump, then drained
2 garlic cloves
1 tsp. dried oregano
1 tbsp. tomato paste
6 tbsp. balsamic vinegar
salt and freshly ground black pepper
½ cup olive oil*

This naturally sweet dressing is excellent when served on strong-flavored salad greens, such as arugula, or on pasta, bruschetta, or small pizza rounds that have been garnished with torn bits of salad greens. Use a high-quality brand of extra virgin olive oil for the finest flavor.

❖ Place the tomatoes, garlic, oregano, tomato paste, and vinegar in a food processor or blender and purée. Add salt and pepper to taste. With the machine running, gradually add the oil in a steady stream until well combined. The dressing will keep for about 3 days in the refrigerator.

Rhineland Dressing

Makes about ¾ cup

INGREDIENTS

*2 tbsp. olive oil
¼ cup apple cider vinegar
¼ cup brandy
salt and freshly ground black pepper*

This is a classic German dressing for vegetables, meat, or fish. With its heady addition of brandy, it can really jazz up leftovers.

❖ Whisk the olive oil, vinegar, and brandy in a small bowl, mixing well to combine. Season with salt and pepper to taste, and serve immediately.

RIGHT *Cal-Ital Sun-dried Tomato Dressing spread on crostini*

34

Section Two

GARDEN VEGETABLE SALADS

❖

Original Caesar

Serves 4

INGREDIENTS

1 egg
2 tbsp. fresh lemon juice
¼ tsp. salt
¼ tsp. freshly ground black pepper
2 tbsp. white wine vinegar
1 clove garlic, peeled and crushed
½ tsp. Dijon mustard
1 tsp. Worcestershire sauce
2 anchovies, finely chopped
½ cup extra-virgin olive oil
1 head romaine lettuce, rinsed, dried, and torn into bite-size pieces and chilled
½ cup freshly grated Parmesan cheese
4 anchovy strips, to garnish

PARMESAN CROUTONS

2 oz. French or Italian-style bread, cubed
1½ tbsp. olive oil
1 large clove garlic
⅛ cup freshly grated Parmesan cheese

Here's a salad that really is fit for movie stars. In the 1920s, Hollywood actors used to dash across the border to Tijuana, Mexico to dine at restaurants owned by an Italian immigrant named Caesar Cardini. He whipped up this extravaganza for them and they began demanding it in restaurants back home. Today, it is served in fine dining establishments the world over.

❖

❖ Cook the egg in its shell in simmering water for about 1½ minutes and set aside until cool enough to handle. In a large bowl combine the salt, pepper, vinegar, garlic, mustard, Worcestershire sauce, and chopped anchovies.

❖ Break the egg into a small bowl and sprinkle the lemon juice over it. Whisk until frothy and pour mixture into the larger bowl containing the salt, pepper, vinegar, garlic, mustard, Worcestershire sauce, and chopped anchovies. Continue whisking while gradually adding in the olive oil.

❖ Make the Parmesan Croutons by heating the oil and garlic in a heavy skillet until the garlic has turned golden. Discard the garlic. Add the bread cubes and cook, stirring for 3–5 minutes until lightly browned; toss cubes in Parmesan cheese.

❖ Add lettuce, cheese, and croutons to the large bowl. Toss gently to coat the salad greens. Place anchovy strips artfully across top of serving bowl or divide salad onto four platters and place an anchovy strip across the top of each. Serve immediately.

Note: Pregnant women and persons with concerns about eggs should substitute pasteurized egg product for the raw egg.

Armenian Eggplant Salad

Serves 4–6

INGREDIENTS
2 eggplants
olive oil for brushing
1 medium onion, chopped
¼ cup finely chopped fresh parsley
2 tsp. salt
1 tsp. black pepper
½ cup olive oil
⅔ cup vinegar
lettuce leaves
tomato wedges or cherry tomatoes and
pitted black olives, to garnish

Eggplant recipes are surprisingly similar the world over. Hungarians like just a hint of sweetness in theirs, so add a pinch of sugar if you find this recipe too tart. The garnishes will add some needed color to the dish.

———————— ❖ ————————

❖ Preheat the broiler to hot. Remove the plant stalk from the eggplant and slice the eggplant into thick rounds. Brush a little olive oil on the eggplant slices, place on a wire rack, and broil for 3–5 minutes on each side, until soft. Let cool, then peel and chop. Mix the eggplant with the onion and parsley in a large bowl. Add the salt and pepper. Whisk the oil and vinegar together in a small bowl, and add to the eggplant mixture. Toss well to coat evenly. Serve the salad on a bed of lettuce leaves, and garnish with tomato wedges or cherry tomatoes and olives.

Sake-soaked Mushrooms

Serves 4

INGREDIENTS
1 cup sake
1½ tbsp. soy sauce
1 tbsp. rice wine vinegar
1 tbsp. sugar
5 large thin slices fresh ginger root
1 large garlic clove, finely chopped
1lb. large mushrooms, rinsed, stemmed,
and thinly sliced
1 tsp. dark sesame oil

This Japanese-style salad makes a light, refreshing accompaniment to broiled meat, fish, and shellfish dishes. The salad will keep well for 2 days in the refrigerator.

———————— ❖ ————————

❖ Combine the sake, soy sauce, rice wine vinegar, sugar, ginger, and garlic in a medium-size nonreactive saucepan. Bring to a boil over a medium heat. Add the mushrooms and reduce the heat to medium-low, simmer for 25 minutes, until the liquid is almost evaporated. Remove from the heat and discard the ginger. Stir in the sesame oil. Set aside to cool to room temperature. Cover, refrigerate, and serve cold.

RIGHT *Armenian Eggplant Salad*

Zesty Asparagus Salad

Serves 4

INGREDIENTS
1lb. asparagus
4–8 large lettuce leaves
1 hard-cooked egg, finely chopped

ZESTY VINAIGRETTE
¼ cup canola or mild olive oil
2 tbsp. red wine vinegar
1 tsp. dry mustard, or 2 tsp. Dijon-style mustard
¼ tsp. black pepper
⅛ tsp. salt
1 large garlic clove, crushed
2 tbsp. snipped fresh chives

The slight sharpness of the mustard in this salad accents the delicate flavor of the asparagus, without overwhelming. It is an adaptation of several French recipes. Use only the hard-cooked egg white if you are concerned about cholesterol. The vinaigrette may be made up to 2 days in advance.

❖

❖ Trim the ends of the asparagus. Soak the stalks in cold water to remove any dirt, then drain. Bring a large flat pan of water to a boil, add the asparagus, and cook for 5–7 minutes until tender-crisp. Alternatively, steam in a large covered pot with about ½-inch boiling salted water for 12–15 minutes. Remove each stalk with tongs. Drain and rinse immediately under cold running water. Drain again, wrap in paper towels, and chill in the refrigerator for about 2 hours.

❖ Prepare the vinaigrette. Place the oil, vinegar, mustard, pepper, salt, garlic, and chives in a jar with a tightly fitting lid, and shake until thoroughly blended. Refrigerate for 2 hours before using.

❖ To serve, line 1–2 lettuce leaves on each of four plates. Divide the chilled asparagus between the plates, and spoon over 1 tbsp. of vinaigrette on each plate. Sprinkle the salads with the hard-cooked egg, and serve.

Classico Italiano

Serves 4

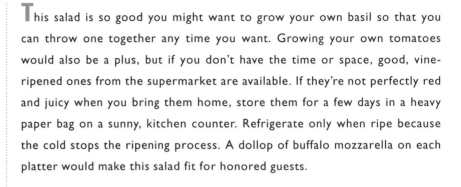

INGREDIENTS
*4 large beefsteak or other sweet, juicy, red
chilled tomatoes, thickly sliced
½ cup extra-virgin olive oil
2–3 tbsp. balsamic, tarragon, or herb
vinegar
salt and freshly ground black pepper
12–16 large sprigs of fresh basil*

This salad is so good you might want to grow your own basil so that you can throw one together any time you want. Growing your own tomatoes would also be a plus, but if you don't have the time or space, good, vine-ripened ones from the supermarket are available. If they're not perfectly red and juicy when you bring them home, store them for a few days in a heavy paper bag on a sunny, kitchen counter. Refrigerate only when ripe because the cold stops the ripening process. A dollop of buffalo mozzarella on each platter would make this salad fit for honored guests.

———————— ❖ ————————

❖ Divide the tomato slices evenly among four salad plates. In a small bowl, whisk the olive oil and vinegar together and season to taste. Arrange basil leaves atop the tomatoes and drizzle with the dressing. Pass extra dressing at the table and an attractive pepper grinder, if you have one.

———————— ————————

Low-cal Coleslaw

Serves 4

INGREDIENTS
*⅓ cup mayonnaise
¼ cup plain non-fat or low-fat yogurt
2 tbsp. cider, rice wine, or
tarragon vinegar
2 tsp. dry mustard
1 tsp. sugar
½ tsp. salt
¼ tsp. Tabasco or other hot pepper sauce
7 cups shredded green cabbage
1 cup chopped red or green bell pepper
2 carrots, peeled and grated
¾ cup sliced scallions*

The name "cole" in coleslaw comes from a Dutch word meaning "cool." For a heartier version of this light salad, add some cauliflower florets and diced zucchini.

———————— ❖ ————————

❖ Mix the mayonnaise, yogurt, vinegar, mustard, sugar, salt, and Tabasco in a medium-size bowl to combine. Add the cabbage, bell pepper, carrots, and scallions and toss well to coat evenly. Cover and refrigerate for up to 3 days. Stir thoroughly before serving.

Moroccan Cucumber Salad

Serves 4

INGREDIENTS
2 large cucumbers
3 tbsp. vinegar
1 garlic clove, crushed
1 tbsp. soy sauce
1 tsp. sesame oil

This cool concoction is a Moroccan specialty and makes a refreshing change from leafy salads.

———————— ❖ ————————

❖ Score the skin of the cucumbers lengthwise with the prongs of a fork, then slice the cucumbers into thin rounds. Put the cucumber slices in a bowl with the vinegar, garlic, and soy sauce, and let stand for several hours in the refrigerator. Stir in the sesame oil just before serving.

Algerian Root-vegetable Salad

Serves 4

INGREDIENTS
1lb. fresh beets
8 oz. small carrots, quartered lengthwise
8 oz. white turnips, pared and cut into
½-inch cubes

DRESSING
½ cup chopped fresh parsley
1 small garlic clove
3 tbsp. white wine vinegar
2 tbsp. olive oil
2 tbsp. apple juice
1½ tsp. drained prepared horseradish
salt and freshly ground black pepper

This salad combines the sharp and sweet flavors of Algerian cuisine, and is a great salad to serve in winter when fresh salad greens and tomatoes are not at their best. It makes an excellent accompaniment to robust meat and poultry dishes.

———————— ❖ ————————

❖ Place beets in a small saucepan and add water to cover. Bring to a simmer and cook for 40 minutes, or until the beets are just tender. Drain well. When cool enough to handle, trim off the stems and slip off the skins under running water. Fill a medium-size stock pot with water and bring to a boil. Add the carrots and turnips. Simmer for 4–6 minutes until just tender. Drain and place in a medium-size bowl.

❖ Prepare the dressing. Place the parsley, garlic, vinegar, olive oil, apple juice, and horseradish in a blender or food processor and blend until well combined. Add salt and pepper to taste.

❖ Toss the beets with half the dressing, toss the carrots and turnips with the remaining half. Mound the beets in the center of a serving plate, and arrange the carrots and turnips in a ring around the beets.

Thai Green Bean Salad

Serves 4 – 6

INGREDIENTS

½ lb. winged beans, yard-long beans, or
green beans
3 tbsp. shredded unsweetened coconut,
fresh or dried
½ cup peanut oil
6 garlic cloves, sliced ⅛-inch thick
lengthwise
¼ cup fresh lime juice
¼ cup unsweetened coconut milk
1 tbsp. roasted chile paste
(ham prik pao)
1 tbsp. Thai fish sauce (nam pla)
1 tbsp. sugar
12 whole radicchio leaves
2 serrano chiles, preferably 1 red and
1 green, seeded and finely chopped

SHALLOT CROUTONS

½ cup peanut oil
4 medium shallots, sliced ⅛-inch thick
cilantro sprigs, to garnish

Finely diced chicken breast or shrimp, or a combination, can be added to this salad to make a hearty lunch-time or supper meal. You can find the unsweetened coconut milk, dried coconut, chile paste, and fish sauce at Asian grocers.

❖

❖ Blanch the beans in a saucepan of boiling, salted water for about 3 minutes, until tender but still crisp. Drain and rinse under cold running water. Cut the beans into bite-size pieces and set aside.

❖ Heat a dry wok or small skillet, add the shredded coconut and toss gently for about 1 minute, until golden. Transfer the coconut to a plate.

❖ Pour the peanut oil into the wok and heat to 375°F using a deep-fat thermometer. Remove the wok from the heat, add the garlic slices, and stir until golden and crisp. Transfer the garlic to paper towels to drain.

❖ In a bowl, whisk together the lime juice and coconut milk. Then whisk in one ingredient at a time: the chile paste, fish sauce, and sugar. Set aside.

❖ Make the shallot croutons by heating the oil in a wok to 375°F (measure using a deep-fat thermometer). Remove the pan from the heat, add the shallots, and stir for about 3 minutes, until the shallots are crisp and golden. Transfer to paper towels to drain. The shallots can be refrigerated, covered, for up to a week, but should then be lightly toasted on a baking sheet in the oven before using.

❖ Arrange the radicchio leaves on a platter or individual plates. In a large bowl, combine the beans, the toasted coconut, and the garlic slices. Pour the mixture of lime juice, coconut milk, chile paste, fish sauce, and sugar over the beans, coconut, and garlic. Gently fold in the serrano chiles.

Jícama Slaw

Serves 4

INGREDIENTS
2 small jícama
½ medium red onion
4 tbsp. Homemade Mayonnaise (see page 29), or any commercial variety
2 tbsp. distilled white vinegar
2 tbsp. Dijon-style mustard
¼ tsp. seeded and finely chopped fresh green serrano chile (optional)
2 tsp. sugar
salt and freshly ground black pepper

The jícama is a delicious root vegetable with a brown skin and white flesh, and it can be served raw or cooked. It has a crunchy texture like water chestnuts. You can find it in Mexican and Caribbean markets. The serrano chile adds spicy pizzazz to the salad, but can be omitted if you prefer.

———— ❖ ————

❖ Peel the jícama. Grate or julienne the vegetable in a food processor, or cut it by hand into matchsticks. Process the onion with the jícama in the food processor , or dice it by hand. Set the jícama and onion aside.

❖ Blend the mayonnaise, vinegar, mustard, chile, and sugar together in a small salad bowl. Stir in the jícama and onion. Add salt and pepper to taste, toss well to combine, and serve.

———— ————

French Mesclun in Herbed Dressing

Serves 4

INGREDIENTS
7 cups loosely packed soft lettuce, such as Boston, bibb, butterhead, Brune d'Hiver, and Four Seasons
1 cup fresh arugula, watercress, or chervil
1 medium cucumber, sliced thinly into rings (remove rind, if you do not like it)

DRESSING
½ cup white tarragon vinegar
½ to 1 tsp. prepared mustard
1¼ cups walnut oil
1 tsp. dry mustard
1½ tsp. fresh basil, finely chopped
1½ tsp. fresh thyme, finely chopped
1½ tsp. fresh sweet marjoram, finely chopped
1½ tsp. fresh chervil, finely chopped
salt and freshly ground black pepper

There seem to be as many French salads as the proverbial 50 million Frenchmen, but here is a true classic that pays homage to fresh ingredients. It is good made with any type of lettuce, but it enhances the delicacy of fresh, soft salad greens. By all means, substitute a prepackaged mix of soft salad greens, if you have discovered a blend you like. Also, you can substitute Continental Herb Dressing (see page 20) if you have some on hand.

———— ❖ ————

❖ In a nonreactive bowl or jar, whisk or shake together the vinegar, prepared mustard, walnut oil, dry mustard, fresh basil, fresh thyme, fresh marjoram, and fresh chervil. Season to taste.

❖ Place greens and cucumber in a serving bowl or divide onto four platters. Drizzle with about half the dressing and toss lightly. Serve and pass the remaining dressing.

Greek Salad

Serves 4

INGREDIENTS

2 tsp. red wine vinegar
½ tsp. sugar
2 tbsp. olive oil
salt and freshly ground black pepper
1 cucumber
3 cups quartered cherry tomatoes
1 cup crumbled feta cheese
½ cup finely chopped fresh basil

This simple, but popular, salad combines crisp cucumber and cherry tomatoes with soft, crumbly feta cheese.

❖

❖ In a large bowl, whisk together the vinegar, sugar, olive oil, and salt and pepper to taste. Peel the cucumber, halve it lengthwise, and remove the seeds. Cut crosswise into ¼-inch slices. Add to the bowl with the tomatoes, feta cheese, and basil. Toss the salad well to combine, and serve.

Italian Salad on Crostini

Serves 4

INGREDIENTS

1 large whole-wheat baguette, cut on the diagonal into 12 slices
2 garlic cloves, peeled and cut in half
1 tbsp. olive oil or vegetable oil
1 sweet yellow bell pepper, cored, seeded, and cut into 1-inch cubes
2 green bell peppers, cored, seeded, and cut into short strips about 1-inch long
1 long fresh red chile, seeded and finely chopped
½ medium onion, thinly sliced
2 medium tomatoes, seeded and cut into 1-inch cubes
1 cup fresh basil leaves, chopped
1 tbsp. chopped fresh oregano
2 tbsp. balsamic or red wine vinegar
¾ tsp. salt
½ tsp. freshly ground black pepper
fresh basil leaves, to garnish

This flavorful salad, spread on toasted bread, makes a nice change from green salads served on a plate or in a bowl. The salad-topped crostini can also be served as an appetizer.

———— ❖ ————

❖ Preheat the broiler. Arrange the bread slices on a broiler pan. Rub garlic cloves on the bread. Discard the garlic. Broil the bread, 3 inches from the heat, for 4 minutes or until browned, turning them over halfway through and watching closely. Arrange three crostini on each of four serving plates.

❖ Heat the oil in a nonstick medium-size skillet over medium heat. Add the yellow and green bell peppers, chile, and onions. Cook, covered, for almost 15 minutes, stirring occasionally. Remove from heat. Stir in the tomatoes, basil, oregano, vinegar, and salt and pepper until combined. Spoon evenly over the crostini, garnish with basil leaves, and serve immediately.

Sweet Potato and Celery Salad

Serves 4

INGREDIENTS

3 lb. sweet potatoes, peeled and cut into ½-inch dice
½ cup white-wine vinegar
⅓ cup Dijon-style mustard
1 cup vegetable oil, or 1 cup of juice extracted from red bell peppers with 1 tbsp. vegetable oil added
2 cups thinly sliced celery
1 cup thinly sliced red bell pepper
1 cup thinly sliced scallions
salt and freshly ground black pepper
lettuce leaves

The sweet potato is often overlooked, but it makes a tasty ingredient in salads. This recipe is adapted from a popular Midwestern salad.

———— ❖ ————

❖ On a rack or steamer basket set over boiling water in a saucepan, steam the sweet potato, covered, for 6–8 minutes, or until tender. Transfer to a bowl and let cool. In a small bowl, whisk together the vinegar and the mustard, then add the oil in a thin stream, whisking until the dressing has emulsified. Pour over the sweet potatoes, add the celery, bell pepper, scallion, and salt and pepper to taste, and mix well to combine. Line four plates with lettuce leaves, top each with one-quarter of the potato salad, and serve.

RIGHT *The makings of Italian Salad on Crostini*

Hearts of Palm Salad

Hearts of Palm Salad

Serves 4

INGREDIENTS
2 tbsp. red wine vinegar
½ cup Dijon-style mustard
salt and freshly ground black pepper
¾ cup canola oil
2 tbsp. walnut oil (optional)
2 7½-oz. cans hearts of palm, drained and
sliced into ½-inch rounds
½ cup roughly broken walnuts

This salad is based on a recipe from Costa Rica, where hearts of palm are harvested. Walnuts, which are usually only imported to Costa Rica at Christmas time, have been added to give the dish a festive touch.

❖

❖ In a small bowl, whisk the vinegar and mustard together to combine. Add salt and pepper to taste. Pour in the canola oil a little at a time, whisking continuously. Stir in the walnut oil. Place the hearts of palm in a bowl with the walnuts, pour over the dressing, and gently toss to coat. Serve immediately.

Asparagus Salad with Fruit-Honey Vinaigrette

Serves 4–6

INGREDIENTS
1lb. asparagus
1 pink grapefruit, peeled and sectioned
with the juice reserved
1 tsp. chopped fresh chives or flat-leaf
parsley
2 tsp. toasted almonds (see page 112)

FRUIT-HONEY VINAIGRETTE
2 tbsp. grapefruit juice, measured out
from the reserved juice
2 tbsp. raspberry vinegar
1 tbsp. honey
⅛ tsp. salt
¼ cup canola oil

This is an elegant dish and a perfect salute to spring. When choosing asparagus, look for tightly closed tips and peel the stalks, if you don't like their texture.

❖

❖ Trim the ends of the asparagus. Soak the stalks in cold water to remove any dirt, then drain. Bring a large flat pan of water to a boil, add the asparagus, and cook for 5–7 minutes until tender-crisp. Alternatively, steam in a large covered pot with about ½-inch boiling salted water for 12–15 minutes. Remove each stalk with tongs. Drain and rinse immediately under cold running water. Drain again, wrap in paper towels, and chill in the refrigerator.

❖ Prepare the vinaigrette. In a small bowl, whisk together the grapefruit juice, raspberry vinegar, honey, and salt. Slowly add the oil and whisk until thickened and blended.

❖ Arrange the asparagus stalks on salad plates and garnish with the grapefruit sections. Drizzle with the vinaigrette, and sprinkle with the chives or parsley and the toasted almonds. Serve immediately.

Russian Dilled Potato Salad

Serves 4

INGREDIENTS
2 tbsp. white wine vinegar
2 tbsp. cider vinegar
1 tbsp. brown sugar
1 tsp. salt
1 tsp. dry chervil (optional)
1 tsp. coarse-grain mustard
2 cups peeled, seeded, and diced cucumber
1 cup plain yogurt
1 cup sour cream
1 tbsp. fresh lemon or lime juice
1 tbsp. dried dill
8 medium new, red potatoes
salt
mild sweet paprika

A Russian immigrant to my home state of Ohio introduced this elegant, yet hearty peasant dish to the region. Substituting non-fat or low-fat sour cream and yogurt will reduce calories and cholesterol with little loss in flavor. The chervil will add a subtle anise flavor, but omit the herb if you do not like its unique taste.

———————— ❖ ————————

❖ In a large nonreactive bowl, mix together the vinegars, brown sugar, salt, chervil, mustard, cucumber, yogurt, sour cream, lemon juice, and dill. Cover and refrigerate.

❖ Wash the potatoes well, gently scrubbing so the skin remains intact. Place potatoes in a large saucepan, cover with water, and bring to a boil. Cook over a medium-high heat for 10–15 minutes, or until tender. Cool under cold running water and drain well. Cut each potato into bite-size pieces. Fold the potatoes into the chilled yogurt and sour cream mixture with a wooden or plastic spoon. Refrigerate for at least 6 hours to let the flavors blend. Season with salt and paprika to taste before serving.

Persian Spinach Salad

Serves 4

INGREDIENTS
1lb. spinach
1 onion, finely chopped
1 tbsp. oil
2 cups yogurt
1 tsp. salt
¼ tsp. pepper
2 garlic cloves, finely chopped
1 tsp. chopped fresh mint
2 tbsp. chopped walnuts

This salad, also called *Borani Esfana*, is creamy, but nutritious, and it is easier to digest than raw spinach salads because the spinach is cooked first.

———————— ❖ ————————

❖ Wash the spinach and roughly chop. Combine with the onion in a saucepan, and blanch in the water which clings to the leaves for about 3 minutes. Drain in the pan, add the oil to the saucepan, and cook for 2 more minutes. Remove from the heat and let cool. Stir in the yogurt, salt, pepper, and garlic, toss with the mint and nuts, and serve.

RIGHT *Russian Dilled Potato Salad*

Section Three

POULTRY AND MEAT SALADS

❖

Antipasto Italiano

Serves 4 – 6

INGREDIENTS
¼ cup ketchup
¼ cup chili sauce
¼ cup water
¼ cup olive oil
¼ cup tarragon wine vinegar
¼ cup fresh lemon juice
¼ garlic clove, finely chopped
½ tbsp. brown sugar
½ tbsp. Worcestershire sauce
½ tbsp. prepared horseradish
dash of cayenne pepper
salt
½ small cauliflower, broken into florets
2 carrots, peeled, sliced into ¼-inch
rounds
1 celery stalk, cut into 1½-inch lengths
4 oz. small whole mushrooms
1 4-oz. jar pepperoncini, drained and
seeded
1 7-oz. can water-packed tuna, drained
1 oz. anchovies, drained
12 green olives, sliced

You can embellish this salad by adding other tidbits, such as artichoke hearts, tiny onions, green beans, or slices of Italian salami and mortadella. You can also use stuffed olives, anchovies, radish roses, or pickled onions for garnishing.

———— ❖ ————

❖ In a 3-quart nonreactive saucepan, combine the ketchup, chili sauce, water, oil, vinegar, lemon juice, garlic, brown sugar, Worcestershire sauce, horseradish, cayenne pepper, and salt to taste. Bring to a boil, then reduce heat and simmer, uncovered, for 2–3 minutes. Add cauliflower florets, carrots, celery, mushrooms, and pepperoncini to the pan. Cover, reduce heat, and simmer slowly for about 20 minutes, until the vegetables are tender-crisp when pierced with a fork. Gently add the tuna in large flakes. Simmer, uncovered, until the tuna is just heated. Spoon onto a divided serving dish, keeping each type of vegetable and the tuna separated. Let cool, and then refrigerate for 2 hours. Garnish with anchovies and olives, and serve.

Floridian King Gasparilla Beef Salad

Serves 4 – 6

INGREDIENTS
1 large head iceberg or 2 bibb or Boston
lettuces, shredded
2 celery stalks, finely chopped
¼ cup finely chopped, salted, dry-roasted
peanuts
2 slices crisply cooked bacon, crumbled
1¼ oz. dried beef, finely shredded
¼ cup chopped carrots
4 oz. Low-fat Blue Cheese Dressing (see
page 29), or a commercial variety

This Floridian salad was created in honor of an annual festival, similar to Mardi Gras, which commemorates the days of pirates and is celebrated with floats, costumes, and frivolity.

———— ❖ ————

❖ In a large bowl, combine the lettuce, celery, peanuts, bacon, beef, and carrots, and mix well. Toss with the dressing and serve immediately.

Monte Cristo Salad

Serves 4

INGREDIENTS

1 tbsp. white wine vinegar

2 tsp. Dijon-style mustard

¼ tsp. dried red pepper flakes

⅛ tsp. freshly ground black pepper

3 oz. cooked lean ham, cut into thin strips

3 oz. cooked turkey or chicken breast, cut into thin strips

1½ oz. Jarlsberg or Muenster cheese, cut into thin strips

1 cup chopped celery

½ cup shredded carrots

½ cup thinly sliced red onion

2 tbsp. chopped parsley

This is named for the sandwich of ham, turkey, and cheese served on French toast. Serve this salad with warm crostini, if desired, to follow through on the theme.

❖

❖ In a large bowl, whisk together the vinegar, mustard, pepper flakes, and black pepper. Add the ham, turkey or chicken, cheese, celery, carrots, onion, and parsley. Toss well to coat. Cover and refrigerate until thoroughly chilled. Stir well before serving.

Mah-jong Club Chicken Salad

Serves 4

INGREDIENTS

2 medium carrots, thinly sliced

½ lb. snow peas

2 tbsp. vegetable oil

2 tbsp. lemon juice

1 tsp. soy sauce

½ tsp. sesame oil

¼ tsp. ground ginger

2 cups cubed cooked chicken breast

1 8-oz. can water chestnuts

4 scallions, thinly sliced

The Chinese flair for combining a variety of textures and tastes comes together in this delightful salad. Served with some sticky rice or a hot-and-sour soup, and garnished with greens and cherry tomatoes, and you have a complete Chinese-style dinner.

❖

❖ Cook carrots in a saucepan of boiling water for about 5 minutes. Add snow peas and cook 1 minute more, or until the vegetables are crisp-tender. Drain and set aside.

❖ Whisk the vegetable oil, lemon juice, soy sauce, sesame oil, and ginger in a serving bowl. Add the chicken, water chestnuts, scallions, and the cooked carrots and snow peas to the bowl. Mix well to coat evenly. Serve at room temperature, or refrigerate for up to 1 hour before serving.

Springtime Chicken Salad

Serves 4

INGREDIENTS

1¼ lb. cooked chicken, skinned, boned, and sliced

1 lb. cooked asparagus

2 oranges, peeled, sectioned, and seeded

lettuce leaves

DRESSING

2 tsp. olive oil

1 tsp. curry powder

1 cup chicken stock

⅓ cup non-fat sour cream

2 tbsp. orange juice

2 tsp. honey

1 tsp. grated orange peel

1 tsp. lemon juice

salt

Inspired by classic chicken salad, this variation marries the citrusy flavor and aroma of oranges with chicken and asparagus. Use reduced-sodium chicken stock, if you are concerned about salt intake.

❖

❖ First prepare the dressing. Heat the oil and curry powder in a small saucepan over a medium-low heat for about 4 minutes. Add the stock and simmer for about 15 minutes, until reduced to ⅓ cup. Whisk in the sour cream, orange juice, honey, orange peel, lemon juice, and salt to taste. Pour into a small heatproof pitcher, and refrigerate for about 2 hours.

❖ After the dressing has chilled, arrange the lettuce leaves on four plates. Top with the chicken, asparagus, and orange sections. Drizzle half the chilled dressing over the salad and pass the rest separately.

RIGHT *Mah-jong Club Chicken Salad*

Dijon Beef Stir-fry Salad

Serves 4

INGREDIENTS
1 tbsp. olive oil
1 lb. beef tenderloin tips, trimmed and cut
into 1½-inch pieces
salt and freshly ground black pepper
10 oz. salad greens

PARMESAN CROUTONS
¼ loaf French or Italian bread
1½ tbsp. extra-virgin olive oil
1 garlic clove, crushed
⅛ cup grated Parmesan cheese

DRESSING
½ cup olive oil
¼ cup Dijon-style mustard
¼ cup balsamic vinegar
1 garlic clove, crushed
1 tsp. sugar

Use your favorite Dijon-style mustard in this dish. I prefer the spicy varieties, but you may like the more mellow, honeyed ones. If you do not have any available, add ¼ cup of honey to any other style of mustard and omit the sugar in the recipe.

❖

❖ Make the dressing by whisking together the olive oil, mustard, vinegar, garlic, sugar, and salt and pepper to taste in a medium-size bowl. Set aside.

❖ In a large nonstick skillet, heat the oil over medium-high heat. Add the beef, a few pieces at a time, and stir-fry for 2–3 minutes, or until browned. Season with a little salt and pepper, and set aside.

❖ In a large bowl, combine the salad greens with half the dressing, tossing to coat.

❖ Now make the croutons. Cut the crusts off the bread, then slice the bread into ½-inch cubes. Heat the oil and garlic in a heavy skillet over a medium heat for 5 minutes, or until the garlic is golden. Discard the garlic. Add the bread cubes and cook, stirring frequently, until lightly browned, 3–5 minutes. Leftover croutons can be stored in a tightly covered jar for up to 3 days. They should be lightly toasted on a baking sheet before using.

❖ Arrange the salad greens on a serving platter, top with the cooked beef, and sprinkle with the croutons. Serve immediately, passing the remaining dressing separately.

Soba Broiled Beef Salad

Serves 4–6

INGREDIENTS

*8 oz. soba noodles, broken into
bite-size pieces*
*8 oz. trimmed broiled steak or cooked roast
beef, thinly sliced and cut into strips*
2 tomatoes, coarsely diced
*1 sweet white onion, peeled, halved
lengthwise, thinly sliced crosswise, and
separated into half-rings*
⅓ cup chopped fresh parsley
⅓ cup chopped fresh basil
2 cups shredded romaine or iceberg lettuce
parsley and cilantro sprigs, to garnish

DRESSING

¼ cup rice wine vinegar
2 tbsp. mayonnaise
2 tbsp. extra-virgin olive oil
½ tsp. dried oregano
½ tsp. ground cumin
1 tsp. salt
¼ tsp. freshly ground black pepper
¼ tsp. ground red chiles

This salad, inspired by Japanese cuisine, can be made with leftover beef. Soba noodles are made from wheat and can be found at many gourmet shops and Asian stores. If you cannot find them, you can substitute linguine, but the result will not be quite as Japanese in style.

———————— ❖ ————————

❖ Make the dressing by whisking together the vinegar, mayonnaise, and olive oil in a large bowl. Then whisk in the oregano, cumin, salt, black pepper, and ground chile until well blended. Set aside. Cook the soba noodles until *al dente*, according to the directions on the package. Drain the noodles well, and add them to the dressing in the bowl. Toss in the beef, tomato, onion, and herbs. Cover and refrigerate for 1–2 hours. Serve on a bed of lettuce, and garnish with parsley and cilantro.

Capered Duck Salad

Serves 4

INGREDIENTS

*14 oz. skinned, boned, roasted duck,
roughly shredded*
*6 oz. boiled potatoes, peeled and cut into
½-inch cubes*
½ cup diced dill pickle
¼ cup chopped scallions
2 tbsp. diced red bell pepper
4 pitted black olives, sliced
*⅓ cup plus 2 tsp. non-fat or low-fat sour
cream*
*1 tbsp. plus 1 tsp. non-fat or low-fat
mayonnaise*
1 tbsp. chopped drained capers
2 tsp. Dijon-style mustard
salt and freshly ground black pepper

This dish combines many of the ethnic influences of American regional cooking. Substitute chicken breast if you do not want the excess calories of duck, which is one of the fattiest meats. This recipe would also work quite well with leftover roast pork.

———————— ❖ ————————

❖ In a medium mixing bowl, combine the duck, potatoes, dill pickle, scallions, bell pepper, and olives. Set aside. In a small bowl, whisk together the sour cream, mayonnaise, capers, and mustard. Season with salt and pepper to taste. Add to the salad just before serving, mixing gently to combine.

Mongolian Beef Salad

Serves 4–6

INGREDIENTS
1½ lb. broccoli
2½ cups thinly sliced mushrooms
2 scallions, thinly sliced
*1 small yellow bell pepper, cut into long,
thin strips*
*1 small red bell pepper, cut into long, thin
strips*
1 small head romaine lettuce
12 radishes, trimmed
1 lb. thinly sliced, cooked roast beef
*toasted sesame seeds, to garnish
(see page 112)*

DRESSING
¼ cup canola or corn oil
¼ cup rice wine vinegar
2 tbsp. soy sauce
2 tsp. dark sesame oil
¼ tsp. garlic powder
¼ tsp. freshly ground pepper

This salad has an Asian flavor, but the ingredients are all easily available. You can prepare the toasted sesame seeds and most of the other ingredients up to a day ahead.

❖

❖ Place all the dressing ingredients in a jar with a tight-fitting lid. Shake vigorously until well blended. Set aside at room temperature to let the flavors develop.

❖ Bring about an inch of lightly salted water to a boil in a large pot. Add the broccoli, cover, and cook for 4–5 minutes, until crisp-tender. Drain in a colander and refresh under cold running water. Drain again, place in a plastic food bag or a lidded container, and refrigerate for 2–24 hours.

❖ In a medium-size bowl, combine the mushrooms and scallions with 2 tbsp. of the dressing. Toss to coat evenly, then place in a sealed plastic bag or a lidded container and refrigerate for 2–24 hours. Refrigerate the remaining dressing.

❖ Remove 12 small leaves from the head of lettuce, and pack them, along with the bell peppers and radishes, in food bags or storage containers. Refrigerate for 2–24 hours.

❖ To serve, line a large platter with lettuce leaves. Roll up the roast-beef slices and arrange them in center of the platter. Spoon the mushroom mixture onto the platter, next to the meat. Arrange the broccoli and bell pepper strips on the other side of the meat, and drizzle with 2 tbsp. of the reserved dressing. Scatter radishes around the platter. Drizzle the remaining dressing over the salad, sprinkle toasted sesame seeds on top, and serve.

Pura Vida Taco Salad

Serves 4 – 6

INGREDIENTS

½ lb. ground beef or turkey, cooked,
crumbled, and drained
2 tbsp. finely chopped canned mild green
chiles
½ 14-oz. can whole peeled tomatoes,
undrained
1 tsp. chili powder
1 tsp. garlic salt
freshly ground black pepper

1 head iceberg or romaine lettuce, torn
into bite-sized pieces
3½ oz. tortilla chips or corn chips
½ cup grated Cheddar cheese
1 cup chopped scallions with green tops
½ medium tomato, coarsely chopped
12 black olives, sliced
sour cream
sliced scallions, to garnish (optional)
2 pickled red chiles, to garnish

Instead of using packaged chips in this recipe, you may like to use soft flour or corn tortillas, baked in a hot oven until they are golden and crispy. You could also substitute low-fat or non-fat sour cream to further reduce the calories in this salad, whose name means "healthy natural life."

---------------- ❖ ----------------

❖ Combine the ground beef or turkey, chiles, whole tomatoes, chile powder, garlic salt, and pepper to taste in a skillet. Mix well with a large wooden spoon and cook over low heat, uncovered, for about 30 minutes, or until most of the moisture has evaporated. Cover and set aside.

❖ Place the lettuce in a large chilled bowl and arrange tortilla chips around the outer edge. Top with the meat mixture and sprinkle cheese, scallions, chopped tomato, and sliced olives around the meat. Top with a dollop of sour cream garnished with scallions and the chiles. Serve immediately.

Cobb Salad

Serves 4 – 6

INGREDIENTS

½ head bibb, Boston, or other soft lettuce, shredded
½ head iceberg lettuce, shredded
½ bunch watercress, cleaned with tough stems discarded
2 large tomatoes, diced
2 cups diced cooked chicken breast
2 avocados, peeled, pitted, and diced
1 large carrot, peeled and shredded
4 slices crisply cooked bacon, crumbled
2 tbsp. chopped scallions
4 oz. Roquefort or gorgonzola cheese, crumbled
2 hard-cooked eggs, finely chopped
10 pitted black olives, sliced
½ cup Classic French Vinaigrette (see page 22)

There are many variations of this classic American layered salad, but it almost always includes romaine lettuce, chicken, a blue cheese, bacon, and hard-cooked eggs. It is said to have been invented at Hollywood's Brown Derby restaurant.

❖

❖ Line a flat salad bowl with the two types of lettuce and the watercress. Arrange the tomato, chicken, and avocado in three separate strips across the bowl. Scatter the carrots and bacon over the salad. Add the scallions and cheese, and then the eggs. Top with the olives. Drizzle with the dressing and serve immediately.

Chef's Salad

Serves 4 – 6

INGREDIENTS

½ tsp. salt
2 tbsp. vinegar
6 tbsp. olive oil
freshly ground black pepper
½ head of iceberg, bibb, or any mild lettuce, finely shredded
white part of 1 scallion, finely chopped
1 cup cooked ham strips, cut ¼-inch wide and 2 inches long
1 cup cooked chicken or turkey strips, cut ¼-inch wide and 2 inches long
1 cup Swiss or Jarlsburg cheese strips, cut ¼-inch wide and 2 inches long
1 tsp. finely chopped fresh parsley
1 tsp. finely chopped fresh basil
1 tsp. finely chopped fresh tarragon
1 medium ripe tomato, cut into ½-inch wedges, to garnish

This popular salad evolved mainly in American hotel restaurants. Today, it is practically a mainstay at every lunch counter in the country. You can substitute beef tongue for the ham, if you prefer.

❖

❖ Whisk together the salt, vinegar, and olive oil. Season with pepper to taste. Put the lettuce and scallion in a large bowl, pour over half the dressing, and toss well to coat. Line the bottom of salad bowl with the dressed lettuce and scallions, and arrange the strips of ham, chicken or turkey, and cheese on top. Pour the remaining dressing over the salad and sprinkle on the herbs. Arrange tomato wedges around the side of the bowl, to garnish, and serve.

LEFT *Cobb Salad*

Section Four

FISH AND
SHELLFISH SALADS

Seared Ahi Salad

Serves 4

INGREDIENTS
1lb. small red-skinned potatoes
2 medium carrots, cut in thin 1½-inch
long matchsticks
1 bowl of ice water
1 medium zucchini, peeled and cut into
1½-inch long matchsticks
1½ lb. tuna steak (or swordfish or bluefish
steak), cut about 1¼ inches thick
salt and freshly ground black pepper
2 tsp. canola or vegetable oil
1lb. bok choy, trimmed and coarsely
chopped
Cilantro-Soy Dressing (see below)
12 Boston or bibb lettuce leaves
12 red oak lettuce leaves
alfalfa sprouts, to garnish
cilantro leaves, to garnish

❖ In a large saucepan, boil the potatoes in salted water for 10–12 minutes, until just tender. Drain and set aside to cool.

❖ Bring a medium-size saucepan of water to a boil. Add the carrots and cook for 1 minute. Drain and transfer the carrots to the bowl of ice water. Repeat this process with the zucchini. Drain the carrots and zucchini, and pat them dry with a paper towel. Place in a medium bowl and set aside.

❖ Heat a large heavy skillet over a high heat for about 5 minutes, until very hot. Slice the tuna on the diagonal in ½-inch thick slices. Season lightly with salt and pepper. Add the oil to the skillet and tilt the pan to coat. Divide the tuna slices into three batches. Add one batch to the skillet and cook for about 1 minute, until the underside of the tuna is browned. Turn the fish over and cook until the other side is browned and the fish is cooked. Using a spatula, transfer the fish to a plate. Repeat with the remaining two batches. Set aside.

❖ Quarter the cooled potatoes, transfer to a large bowl, and add the carrots, zucchini, and bok choy. Toss with 6 tbsp. of the Cilantro-Soy Dressing. Season with salt and pepper to taste. Arrange 3 leaves of the Boston or bibb lettuce, and 3 leaves of the red oak lettuce on each plate. Mound one-quarter of the dressed vegetables on top of the lettuce in the center of each plate. Divide the tuna slices between the plates, arranging them around the vegetables. Garnish with the sprouts and cilantro. Pass the remaining dressing separately.

Cilantro-Soy Dressing

Makes about ½ cup

INGREDIENTS
2-inch piece ginger root, peeled
3 tbsp. fresh lime juice
3 tbsp. soy sauce
1 tbsp. sesame oil
1 tsp. minced garlic
dash of cayenne pepper
¼ cup corn oil
1 tsp. finely chopped fresh cilantro

Make this dressing up to 3 hours ahead; cover and refrigerate.

———————— ❖ ————————

❖ Grate the ginger root on a small grater. Squeeze the ginger through a garlic press held over a small bowl. Measure out 1 tbsp. of the ginger juice and transfer to a small nonreactive bowl. Add the lime juice, soy sauce, sesame oil, garlic, and cayenne pepper to the bowl. Gradually whisk in the vegetable oil, in a fine stream, until blended. Stir in the cilantro.

72

Hungarian Herring Salad

Serves 4 – 6

INGREDIENTS

2 pickled herrings
3 hard-cooked eggs
2 medium-size boiled potatoes
2 red apples, cored and seeded
1 tbsp. chopped onion
¼ cup vinegar
¼ cup olive oil
½ tsp. prepared mustard
salt
mild sweet paprika

Some of the most wonderful herring dishes come from Hungary, where fish has been pickled for centuries. The apples add a touch of sweetness and a crunchy texture.

❖

❖ Slice the herring into small pieces, and place in a large serving dish. Dice the eggs, potatoes, and apples, and add to the dish with the onion. In a small bowl, blend the vinegar, oil, and mustard together, and season to taste with the salt and paprika. Pour over the salad, and toss gently to coat. Let stand for 30 minutes before serving, then sprinkle with a little paprika to add a dash of color.

73

Japanese Shrimp Salad

Serves 4

INGREDIENTS

12 oz. bean sprouts
1 bunch watercress, washed with tough stems discarded
8 medium cooked and chilled shrimp, shelled and cut into quarters
2 tbsp. crushed toasted sesame seeds (see page 112)
2 tbsp. soy sauce
1 tbsp. vinegar
1 tbsp. sesame oil
1 tsp. sugar

Here's a shrimp salad with the tastes and textures of Japanese cuisine.

❖

❖ Half-fill a 5- or 6-quart kettle with water. Bring to a boil over a high heat. Drop in the bean sprouts and cook for 30 seconds. Drain, rinse with cold water, and drain again. Cover and refrigerate until cold.

❖ Tear the watercress into 2-inch lengths, and place in a serving bowl with the bean sprouts, shrimp, and sesame seeds. Stir the soy sauce, vinegar, sesame oil, and sugar together in a small bowl. Pour over the salad, toss until well coated, and serve.

Salmon Mousse

Serves 4

INGREDIENTS

½ 8-oz. can sockeye salmon, drained
1½ tbsp. lemon juice
½ cup dairy sour cream
4 oz. cream cheese, softened
¼ cup mayonnaise
⅛ cup chili sauce
⅛ tsp. Tabasco or other hot pepper sauce
1 tsp. Worcestershire sauce
¼ tsp. salt
¼ tsp. white pepper
1 ¼-oz. envelope unflavored gelatin
⅛ cup cold water
¼ cup boiling water
¼ cup finely chopped green bell pepper
¼ cup finely chopped celery
¼ cup finely chopped scallions
butter, for greasing
parsley sprigs, to garnish

Some of the best sockeye, or red, salmon comes from British Columbia's Fraser River and Alaska's Copper River.

❖

❖ Remove any skin and bones from the salmon. Sprinkle the salmon with the lemon juice, and set aside.

❖ In a food processor, or with an electric mixer, combine the sour cream, cream cheese, and mayonnaise. Add chili sauce, Tabasco, Worcestershire sauce, salt, and white pepper. Mix well and set aside.

❖ Soften the gelatin in the cold water, then add boiling water and stir to dissolve the gelatin. Let cool, then add to the cream cheese mixture in food processor and mix well. Add the salmon to the food processor and process until just combined. Fold in the bell pepper, celery, and scallions.

❖ Pour into a greased 2-quart mold. Cover and refrigerate overnight. Unmold and garnish with parsley sprigs.

RIGHT *Japanese Shrimp Salad*

74

Salmon and Potato Salad with Horseradish Dressing

Serves 4

INGREDIENTS
1½ lb. small waxy potatoes
salt
1 large bunch of watercress, cleaned with
tough stems discarded
olive oil cooking spray
¾-lb. salmon fillet, cut into thin slices on
the diagonal
freshly ground black pepper

HORSERADISH DRESSING
1 cup low-fat buttermilk
2 scallions, coarsely chopped
¼ cup prepared horseradish, drained
salt and freshly ground black pepper

Ask your fish dealer to slice the salmon for you, if you feel uneasy about slicing it yourself.

❖

❖ Cover the potatoes with cold water in a medium saucepan and add 1 tsp. salt. Bring to a boil over a moderately high heat and cook for about 20 minutes, until the potatoes are tender. Drain the potatoes and slice them crosswise in ¼-inch thick slices. When cooled, place the potatoes in a bowl with the watercress.

❖ Make the dressing by stirring the buttermilk, scallions, and horseradish together in a small bowl. Season with salt and pepper to taste. Add half the dressing to the potatoes and watercress, and toss to coat. Arrange the salad on four large plates, and drizzle with the remaining dressing.

❖ Lightly coat a broiling pan or large nonstick skillet with cooking spray and heat. Season the salmon with salt and pepper, add to the skillet, and sear over a high heat, without turning, for about 30 seconds, until browned on the bottom. Remove from the pan or skillet, and arrange, browned sides up, on the salads. Serve immediately.

Luscious Lobster Salad

Serves 4

INGREDIENTS
2 lobsters, about 1¼ lb. each
4–6 cups torn mixed salad greens

COURT BOUILLON
2 carrots, scrubbed and sliced
2 celery stalks, sliced
1 leek, sliced
1 sprig of fresh thyme
1 bay leaf
1 tsp. salt
½ tsp. white pepper
2 quarts water
2 cups dry white wine

FRUIT VINAIGRETTE
6 tbsp. walnut oil
¼ cup balsamic vinegar
½ mango or 4 fresh peaches, diced
2 shallots, diced, or 2 tbsp. chopped red onion
¼ cup diced red bell pepper
¼ cup whole cilantro leaves
salt and white pepper

Using white pepper in the court bouillon and the vinaigrette maintains the pristine look of the velvety, white lobster meat in this adaptation of a classic French salad.

————————— ❖ —————————

❖ Place all the court bouillon ingredients in a tall lobster pot. Bring to a boil over a high heat and continue to boil for 20 minutes. Add the lobsters to the pot and return to a boil for 12 minutes, until the shells have turned bright red. Using tongs, remove the lobsters from the pot. The bouillon can be reserved for use in a seafood stew or another dish. When the lobsters are cool enough to handle, remove the meat from the claws and tail. To do this, twist off the claws and crack them to extract the meat. For each lobster, separate the tail from the head and body. Cut down the center length of the underside of the tail, bend apart, and remove the meat. Discard the head and body. Slice the tail meat crosswise, and set aside.

❖ Make the vinaigrette by mixing the oil, vinegar, mango or peaches, shallots or onion, bell pepper, and cilantro leaves in a small bowl. Season with salt and white pepper to taste, and set aside.

❖ Divide the salad greens between four plates and spoon three-quarters of the vinaigrette over them. Arrange the lobster meat on top of the greens, spoon over the remaining vinaigrette, and serve.

Mediterranean Tuna and White Bean Salad

Serves 4

INGREDIENTS

2 6½-oz. cans water-packed tuna, drained and flaked
⅓ cup chopped red onion or scallions
4 medium tomatoes, chopped
½ cup chopped fresh basil
2 tbsp. finely chopped fresh parsley
2 15-oz. cans cannellini beans, rinsed and well drained
1½ cups cooked pasta shapes or elbow macaroni
romaine lettuce or fresh spinach leaves (optional)

DRESSING

4 tbsp. capers
5 tbsp. red wine vinegar
1 tbsp. balsamic vinegar
2 garlic cloves, crushed
¼ tsp. salt
¼ tsp. freshly ground black pepper
3–4 tbsp. extra-virgin olive oil

This wonderful concoction combines the delicate flavor of cannellini beans with tuna. The Italian white kidney beans are available in dry and canned forms. Use the best quality of extra-virgin olive oil you can find to ensure successful results.

———————— ❖ ————————

❖ In a jar with a tight-fitting lid, combine capers, red wine vinegar, balsamic vinegar, garlic, salt, pepper, and olive oil. Cover, shake well, and set aside for 1–2 hours to let the flavors blend.

❖ In a large serving bowl, combine the tuna, onion, tomatoes, basil, parsley, beans, and pasta. Just before serving, pour the dressing over the salad, toss gently to coat, and serve on a bed of lettuce or spinach leaves.

Warm Shrimp and Sesame Salad

Serves 4

INGREDIENTS

2 heads endive, cored and leaves separated
1 small head radicchio, leaves separated
2 small heads bibb lettuce, leaves separated
1 lb. shrimp, shelled and deveined with tails left on
1 tbsp. olive oil
2 tbsp. finely chopped scallions
2 tsp. finely chopped garlic
2 tsp. grated fresh pared ginger root spinach leaves
2 cups halved cherry tomatoes
4 tbsp. toasted sesame seeds (see page 112)

DRESSING

½ cup dry sherry
3 tbsp. lemon juice
2 tbsp. olive oil
1 tbsp. sugar
2 garlic cloves, minced
½ tsp. finely chopped fresh rosemary
salt and freshly ground black pepper

This salad combines several textures, colors, and flavors. It is served warm to bring out the full toasty, nutty crunchiness of the sesame seeds.

— ❖ —

❖ Place endive, radicchio, and bibb lettuce in a large salad bowl. Cover and refrigerate until serving time. Make the dressing by combining the sherry, lemon juice, olive oil, sugar, garlic, rosemary, and salt and pepper to taste in a jar with a tight-fitting lid and shaking well. Refrigerate until ready to assemble the salad.

❖ Pat the shrimp dry with a paper towel. Heat the olive oil in large skillet over a high heat. Add the shrimp and cook, stirring, until just pink and lightly browned. Remove the skillet from heat and quickly add the scallions, garlic, and ginger. Toss constantly until the scallions are wilted and the mixture is fragrant. Let cool to room temperature.

❖ To serve, line four plates with the spinach leaves. Gently toss the chilled salad greens with the dressing, and divide between the plates. Top each plate with one-quarter of the shrimp mixture. Arrange ½ cup of tomatoes on each plate, and sprinkle the salads with toasted sesame seeds.

Hawaiian Shrimp-Chayote Salad

Serves 4

INGREDIENTS
½ cup fresh orange juice
¼ cup fresh lime juice
¾ cup vegetable or almond oil, or red
pepper juice with 1 tsp. almond oil added
salt and freshly ground black pepper
1 quart mixed salad greens, torn into
small pieces and chilled
½ lb. cooked shrimp, shelled
2 chayotes, peeled and julienned
2 tbsp. capers
Maui or Vidalia onion rings, to
garnish (optional)

This salad draws on Hawaiian cuisine for inspiration. Red pepper juice is a Hawaiian ingredient and can be obtained by extracting the juice from red bell peppers. If you can find one of the sweet Maui or Vidalia onions, you can garnish the platters with onion rings. The onions have a high sugar content and taste delicious in salads.

———————— ❖ ————————

❖ In a small saucepan, boil the orange and lime juices over a high heat for about 5 minutes, until reduced by half. Transfer to a bowl, let cool, cover, and refrigerate until well chilled. Whisk in the oil or red pepper juice, and season with salt and pepper to taste. Put the chilled salad greens in a large serving bowl, and strew the chayote on top. If the shrimp are small, leave them whole; if they are medium-size, slice them through the center lengthwise; if large, slice them through the center and then cut across, making each shrimp into four pieces. Add the shrimp to the salad and sprinkle with the capers. Pour the dressing over and serve.

Italian Bean and Tuna Salad

Serves 4

INGREDIENTS
1 red onion, very thinly sliced
2 tbsp. white wine vinegar
3–4 tbsp. red wine vinegar
2 cups cooked or canned white beans or
cranberry beans
1 6½-oz. can water-packed tuna, drained.
2 tomatoes, diced
1 garlic clove, minced
juice of 1 lemon
3–4 tbsp. chopped fresh basil or parsley
1 tsp. chopped fresh sage
2 tbsp. olive oil
1 tbsp. plain low-fat yogurt
1 tbsp. capers
salt and freshly ground black pepper
2 tomatoes, cut into wedges, to garnish
romaine lettuce leaves (optional)

Italians usually eat their beans warm, but this salad has such authentic flavors that I think even Italians would adore it. Substitute a naturally sweet Vidalia or Maui onion for the red onion if you can find them.

———————— ❖ ————————

❖ To make the onion sweeter, toss the onion slices with the white-wine vinegar in a bowl, and add water to cover. Let soak for 30 minutes, then drain. In a large bowl, toss together the remaining ingredients, except the tomato wedges and lettuce. Line a bowl, or platter with the lettuce, top with the salad, garnish with the tomatoes, and serve.

RIGHT *Hawaiian Shrimp-Chayote Salad*

Niçoise Salad

Serves 4 – 6

INGREDIENTS

1 head Boston lettuce
¾ cup Classic French Vinaigrette (see page 22), or a commercial variety
2 cups cooked French-cut green beans
2 cups diced cooked potatoes
1 cup drained and flaked canned tuna
2–3 tomatoes, peeled and quartered
2 hard-cooked eggs, quartered
6 anchovies, cut in half
1 tbsp. chopped fresh tarragon, chervil, or parsley

This famous salad from France makes a wonderful, refreshing lunch or dinner on a warm day.

❖ ─────── ❖ ───────

❖ Wash and dry the lettuce, tear into small pieces, and put in a salad bowl. Sprinkle a few tablespoons of the French dressing over the top. Arrange the beans, potatoes, and tuna on top of the salad greens, and place the tomatoes around the edge of the bowl. Top with the eggs and anchovies. Pour over the remaining dressing, sprinkle with fresh tarragon, chervil, or parsley, and serve.

Tres Colores Ceviche de Mexico

Serves 4

INGREDIENTS

1½ lb. red snapper fillets, skin removed
¼ tsp. pickling salt
½ tsp. freshly ground black pepper
1 large red bell pepper, cut into very thin rings
1 large green bell pepper, cut into very thin rings
1 large yellow bell pepper, cut into very thin rings
1 red onion, very thinly sliced
1 cup fresh lemon juice
½ cup fresh lime juice
3 tbsp. tequila
unsalted butter
kosher salt
2 tbsp. chopped fresh cilantro, to garnish

This tri-colored salad, influenced by Mexican cuisine, is bright with yellow, red, and green bell peppers. The snapper is cured by the acidic lime and lemon juices. If you are worried about uncooked seafood, poach or steam the snapper first, then chill the fish, and proceed with the recipe.

─────── ❖ ───────

❖ Arrange the snapper fillets in single layer in a large glass dish. Season with the pickling salt and pepper. Cover with the sliced bell peppers and onion. Pour the lemon juice, lime juice, and tequila over it, and cover with plastic wrap. Marinate in the refrigerator, turning occasionally, for about 36 hours, until the fish is almost opaque.

❖ Rub a small amount of butter around the rims of four glass serving plates. Roll the rims in kosher salt, as you would a margarita glass. Place the plates in the refrigerator for about 5 minutes, until the salted rims harden.

❖ Drain the snapper and cut it into 1-inch cubes. Arrange one-quarter of the bell pepper and onion rings on each plate, then mound one-quarter of the fish in the center of each plate. Garnish with cilantro and serve.

Luxurious Crab Louis

Serves 4

INGREDIENTS

½ head iceberg lettuce, shredded, or
¼ cup shredded mixed lettuces
2 cups flaked fresh crabmeat
1 cup Homemade Mayonnaise
(see page 29)
⅓ cup whipped cream
2 tsp. Worcestershire sauce
1 tsp. chopped fresh dill
2–3 tbsp. chili sauce
2–3 tbsp. grated onion
¼ cup chopped green bell pepper
1–3 tbsp. chopped fresh parsley
cayenne pepper
3–4 hard-cooked eggs, quartered
3–4 tomatoes, cut into wedges
6–8 small bottled artichoke hearts, or
frozen artichoke hearts, thawed

Food writer, historian, and biographer Evan Jones has traced this salad to Solari's, a San Francisco restaurant that served it as early as 1914. This dish is luxurious, combining rich-tasting crabmeat, artichokes, and cream.

❖

❖ Divide the lettuce among four plates. Place one-quarter of the crabmeat on top of lettuce on each plate. In a small bowl, mix the mayonnaise with the cream, Worcestershire sauce, dill, chili sauce, onion, green bell pepper, and parsley, and add cayenne pepper to taste. Spread one-quarter liberally over the crabmeat on each plate and top with eggs, tomato wedges, and artichoke hearts.

South American Mussel Salad

Serves 4

INGREDIENTS

5½ lb. mussels
salt
baking soda or flour
¼ cup olive oil
⅛ cup sherry vinegar
½ tsp. lemon juice
½ garlic clove, peeled and finely chopped
½ serrano or jalapeño chile, seeded and finely chopped

¼ tsp. ground fennel
½ tsp. coarse salt
½ medium red onion, peeled and thinly sliced
1 medium fennel bulb, thinly sliced
¼ cup finely chopped flat-leaf parsley
½ tsp. finely chopped fresh dill

Buy mussels with tightly closed shells or shells that close tightly when tapped. Gaping shells indicate that the shellfish are dead and definitely not edible. Keep the mussels cold until you are ready to prepare them. The mussels can be served in their shells if preferred.

❖

❖ Scrub the mussels with a brush under cold running water to remove all the sand and mud from the shells. Rinse and place in a solution of ⅓ cup salt per gallon of water with 1 tbsp. baking soda or a sprinkling of flour. Leave to soak for about 2 hours. Discard any mussels that float, or are broken or damaged. Rinse again. Pull out and cut off the string beards from each mussel. Drain and set aside.

❖ Place the mussels in a skillet or sauté pan with a tight-fitting lid, and add 1 cup of water. Cover the saucepan and steam the mussels over high heat for about 5 minutes. Discard any mussels that have not opened. Transfer the mussels to a bowl using a slotted spoon. Discard the liquid. When the mussels are cool enough to handle, gently pull off any remaining beards and remove the mussels, intact, from their shells; discard the shells.

❖ In a large bowl, mix together the olive oil, vinegar, lemon juice, garlic, chile, ground fennel, salt, onion, fennel, and parsley. Toss well and adjust the seasoning by adding salt, if necessary. Add the mussels to the bowl, toss again, and transfer to a serving dish. Sprinkle with the chopped dill and serve.

Section Five

Grain, Bean, and Pasta salads

Mama Mia's Pasta Salad

Serves 4

INGREDIENTS

1 lb. dried pasta shapes, such as rotini, penne, fusilli, or shells

½ cup (about 1 oz.) sun-dried tomatoes, soaked in hot water for 5 minutes, then drained

½ lb. smoked mozzarella, cut into ½-inch cubes

1 1-lb. can garbanzo beans, drained and rinsed

10–20 small strips of bottled pepperoncini

½ tsp. dried red pepper flakes

1 loosely packed cup fresh, flat-leaf parsley leaves

DRESSING

2 garlic cloves

1 tbsp. Dijon-style mustard

⅓ cup red wine vinegar

2 tbsp. balsamic vinegar

1 tbsp. water

½ cup olive oil, or ½ cup of juice extracted from red bell peppers with 2 tsp. of vegetable oil added

salt

While chock-full of Italian ingredients, this pasta salad, like most pasta salads, is American. Italians prefer their noodles warm, but Americans have been eating the cold ones since the macaroni salad was created in the early 1900s. This is a great salad to make the day after you have a party, because you can embellish the salad with leftover cold cuts, such as hard salami, pastrami, or ham.

❖

❖ Cook the pasta in a large pot of boiling salted water until *al dente*, then rinse under cold running water and drain well. Transfer the pasta to a very large bowl.

❖ Make the dressing by combining the garlic, mustard, vinegars, water, and oil in a blender or food processor, and blending until smooth. Add salt to taste. Pour the dressing over the pasta and toss to coat evenly. Stir in the sun-dried tomatoes, mozzarella, garbanzo beans, pepperoncini, red pepper flakes, and parsley. Cover and refrigerate for 4 hours; make sure the mixture is thoroughly chilled before serving.

Tex-Mex Corn and Black Bean Salad

Serves 6 – 8

INGREDIENTS

1 12-oz. can whole-kernel corn, drained
with juice reserved
1 15-oz. can black beans, drained and rinsed
1 red bell pepper, finely chopped
½ cup chopped scallions
½ cup chopped red onion
1 garlic clove, finely chopped
1 medium tomato, chopped
1 jalapeño chile, seeded and finely
chopped (optional)
cilantro sprigs or red onion wedges, to
garnish

DRESSING

¼ cup corn juice, measured out from the
reserved juice
¼ cup red wine vinegar
¼ cup olive oil
¾ tsp. Tabasco or other hot pepper sauce
½ tsp. chile powder
1 tbsp. fresh lemon or lime juice
1 tbsp. chopped fresh cilantro

This healthy salad has only the smallest amount of oil in it, with the juice from the corn used as a substitute for part of the oil. Unlike some other Tex-Mex bean dishes, this one does not depend on fat for flavor, and it is nutritious and low in calories.

———————— ❖ ————————

❖ In a large bowl, combine the corn, beans, bell pepper, scallion, red onion, garlic, tomato, and jalapeño. Set aside.

❖ To make the dressing, place the corn juice, vinegar, olive oil, Tabasco or pepper sauce, chile powder, lemon or lime juice, and cilantro in a jar with a tight-fitting lid. Tighten the lid and shake to mix well. Pour the dressing over the salad and stir to mix. Cover and refrigerate for at least 6 hours, or overnight. To serve, transfer the salad to an attractive bowl and garnish with a few sprigs of cilantro or thin wedges of red onion.

Three-bean Salad in a Cilantro Dressing

Serves 4–6

INGREDIENTS
½ lb. dried black beans, rinsed
½ lb. dried white beans, rinsed
1 garlic clove
1 bottle of pickled jalapeño chiles, drained
and with chiles seeded, if desired
1 loosely packed cup fresh cilantro leaves
¼ cup fresh lemon juice
½ cup plus 1 tbsp. canola or vegetable oil
salt
½ lb. green beans, trimmed and cut into
1-inch pieces

This salad takes a little time to make, but the flavor is so much more robust than canned three-bean salads that it is worth the trouble. You may want to double the recipe, so you can serve it again. The salad will keep, covered, in the refrigerator for about one week.

❖

❖ Place the black beans in a large saucepan, and add triple their volume of cold water. In another large saucepan, place the white beans with the same proportion of cold water. Bring the water to a boil in both pans and simmer the beans, uncovered, for 2 minutes. Remove the pans from the heat, and let the beans soak for 1 hour. Drain each pan of beans separately through a colander. Refill each pan with 1¼ quarts water. Stir the black beans into the water in one pan, and the white beans into the water in the other. Cook the beans at a low simmer, testing for tenderness every 5 minutes for 15–40 minutes: they are cooked when they are just tender but still hold their shape. Drain the beans and let them cool slightly.

❖ In a blender, purée half a garlic clove, the jalapeños, and half the cilantro with half the lemon juice, ½ cup of the oil, and salt to taste, scraping down the side of the blender, until the dressing is smooth. Transfer the cooked beans to a very large bowl, and toss with the dressing. Cover, refrigerate, and leave them to marinate overnight, stirring occasionally.

❖ The next day, boil the green beans in a saucepan of boiling, salted water for 5 minutes, or until they are crisp-tender. Drain, refresh under cold water, and pat them dry. In a blender, purée the remaining half a garlic clove with the remaining cilantro, and oil, adding salt to taste and scraping down the side of the blender until the dressing is smooth. Add the green beans and the dressing to the bowl of dressed beans, toss the salad well, and serve it at room temperature.

Garbanzo Bean and Cherry Tomato Salad

Serves 4

INGREDIENTS

1 garlic clove, lightly crushed
2 tbsp. olive oil
1 tbsp. lemon juice
⅛ tsp. salt
⅛ tsp. pepper
1 16-oz. can garbanzo beans, drained and rinsed
1 cup halved cherry tomatoes
¼ cup finely chopped scallions
lettuce leaves, to serve (optional)

This recipe is inspired by Indian salads, but uses ingredients that are readily available. The salad makes a wonderful accompaniment for Indian or Mediterranean dishes.

❖

❖ Rub the inside of a medium-size serving bowl with the crushed garlic. Discard the garlic. Whisk the oil, lemon juice, salt, and pepper in the bowl. Add the garbanzo beans, tomatoes, and scallion. Cover and refrigerate for up to 24 hours, stirring occasionally. Serve on a bed of lettuce, if desired.

Caldo Gallego Salad

Serves 4

INGREDIENTS

1 carrot, peeled and thinly sliced
2 tbsp. olive oil
2 tbsp. lemon juice
¾ tsp. ground dried sage
⅛ tsp pepper
1 15-oz. can cannellini beans, drained and rinsed
4oz. baked ham, cut into ¼-inch cubes
1 celery stalk, thinly sliced
¼ cup chopped red onion
lettuce leaves, to serve (optional)

This salad is inspired by the famous Galician soup of Spain, a dish that is also popular with Cubans and other Spanish-speaking groups of the Americas and Caribbean. The combination of velvety cannellini beans and ham works just as well in a salad as in a soup.

❖

❖ Boil the carrot for 3–5 minutes, until lightly cooked. Drain and set aside. Whisk the oil, lemon juice, sage, and pepper together in a medium-size bowl. Add the cooked carrot, beans, ham, celery, and onion. Refrigerate for up to 1 hour before serving, if desired, and serve on a bed of lettuce.

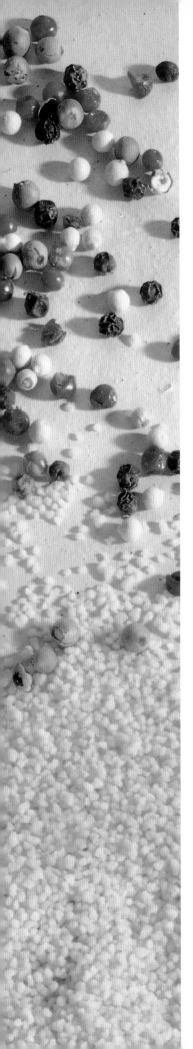

Tabbouleh

Serves 4

INGREDIENTS

½ cup chicken stock
½ cup water
¼ cup fresh lemon juice
¼ cup olive oil
¾ cup couscous, made of wheat semolina, or bulghur wheat
½ seedless cucumber, cut into ¼-inch pieces

2 tbsp. peeled, seeded, and finely diced tomato
½ cup finely chopped scallions
salt
1 tsp. chopped fresh basil
1 loosely packed cup chopped fresh parsley
½ loosely packed cup chopped fresh mint
mint sprigs and cucumber slices, to garnish

The Phoenician Resort in Scottsdale, Arizona, combines this popular grain salad with gingery crab. Although this is a simpler recipe, you may like to add seafood or other ingredients. The salad may be made 2 days ahead, kept covered in the refrigerator.

❖

❖ In a saucepan, combine the stock, water, half the lemon juice, and 1 tablespoon of the oil. Bring the mixture to a boil and stir in the couscous. Cover the pan, remove it from the heat, and let the couscous stand for 5 minutes. Fluff the couscous with a fork and let it cool in the pan.

❖ In a large bowl, stir together the cucumber, tomato, scallion, the remaining olive oil, the remaining lemon juice, and salt to taste. Let the mixture stand for 15 minutes. Add the couscous and herbs, stirring well to mix. Cover the salad and refrigerate for 1 hour before serving.

Old California Inn Rice Salad

Old California Inn Rice Salad

Serves 4

INGREDIENTS
1¼ cups chicken stock
½ cup long-grain white rice, uncooked
1 6-oz. jar artichoke hearts
2 scallions, chopped
¼ cup, sliced pimento-stuffed green olives
½ medium green bell pepper, diced
1 celery stalk, diced
1 tbsp. chopped fresh parsley
¼ tsp. curry powder
¼ cup mayonnaise
salt and freshly ground black pepper

This salad is adapted from a recipe served at an old stagecoach stop in California in the Santa Ynez valley, northwest of Santa Barbara.

❖ Bring the chicken stock to a boil in a large saucepan. Add the rice and return to the boiling point. Reduce heat, cover, and simmer for 20 minutes, or until all the liquid is absorbed. Transfer the rice to a large serving bowl and let cool.

❖ Drain the artichoke hearts, reserving the liquid for the dressing. Chop the artichoke hearts. Add the artichokes, scallions, olives, green pepper, celery, and parsley to the cooled rice. To make the dressing, mix together the reserved artichoke liquid, curry powder, and mayonnaise in a small bowl. Season with salt and pepper to taste. Pour the dressing over the rice salad and mix well to combine. Refrigerate before serving.

Capellini and Chilled Tomato Salad

Serves 4–6

INGREDIENTS
8 oz. dried capellini or spaghettini
3 large, ripe tomatoes, peeled, seeded, chopped, and thoroughly drained of juices
4 garlic cloves, finely chopped
5 black olives, pitted and finely chopped
1 small hot chile, seeded and finely chopped
1 tbsp. olive oil
juice of 1 lime
1 tbsp. chopped fresh cilantro
⅛ tsp. salt
freshly ground black pepper

This salad combines the wonderful, sweet flavor of ripe tomatoes with the sass of chile and other spices.

❖ Cook the capellini according to the directions on the package and until *al dente*. Rinse, drain well, and set aside. Mix the tomatoes and garlic together in a large bowl, then toss in the drained pasta. Refrigerate to chill thoroughly.

❖ In a separate bowl, mix the olives, chile, olive oil, lime juice, cilantro, and salt together to combine thoroughly. Add pepper to taste and set aside. Just before serving, pour the dressing over the pasta, and toss to mix well.

Thai Noodle Salad in a Peanut Dressing

Serves 4

INGREDIENTS
1lb. thin oriental noodles
½ lb. snow peas
1 red bell pepper, cut into strips
1 medium or 2 small cucumbers, thinly sliced
4 scallions, cut diagonally into thin slices
1 cup shredded bok choy

PEANUT DRESSING
½ cup creamy peanut butter
½ cup plain non-fat yogurt
1 tbsp. low-sodium soy sauce
1 garlic clove
2 tbsp. dark sesame oil
3 tbsp. chopped cilantro
2 tbsp. rice wine vinegar

The variety of textures in this dish is typical of Thai cuisine. The combination of noodles and crunchy vegetables in a nutty dressing ensures an exciting eating experience.

❖

❖ Cook the noodles in a large pot of boiling water according to the package directions, until they are tender. Drain well, transfer to a large serving bowl, and set aside. (If you are working ahead of time, toss with 1 tbsp. vegetable oil.)

❖ Trim stem ends of the snow peas and blanch them in boiling water for about 1 minute. Drain well and rinse in cold water; they should be bright green in color. Add the snow peas, red bell peppers, cucumber, and scallions to the noodles, and toss to mix. Add the bok choy and toss again gently.

❖ In a large nonreactive bowl stir together the peanut butter, yogurt, soy sauce, garlic, sesame oil, cilantro, and vinegar. Add the dressing to the salad, toss again, and serve.

Bean and Rice Medley

Serves 4 – 6

INGREDIENTS
2 cups cooked or canned black or red beans, such as Colorado or cranberry, rinsed and drained
2 cups cooked rice.
1½ cups chopped fresh cilantro
¼ cup fresh lime juice
¼ cup olive oil
½ cup chopped onion
2 garlic cloves, crushed
salt and freshly ground black pepper

This dish, originally from Florida, is made in Key West with Key lime juice, but Persian or any other lime juice will work just as well.

❖

❖ Mix the beans, rice, and cilantro together in a large bowl. Place the lime juice in a small bowl and whisk in the oil a little at a time until well blended. Add the onion and garlic to the dressing and pour over the salad, tossing to mix well. Add salt and pepper to taste, mix again, and serve.

LEFT *Ingredients for Thai Noodle Salad in a Peanut Dressing*

Caponata Rice Salad

Serves 4–6

INGREDIENTS

1 tbsp. salt
1½ cups arborio rice
1 medium onion, cut into ¼-inch dice
6 tbsp. olive oil
1 small eggplant, cut into ½-inch dice
2 garlic cloves, finely chopped
3 tbsp. balsamic vinegar
3 large ripe tomatoes, seeded and cut into
½-inch dice

2 tbsp. drained capers
¼ cup coarsely chopped, pitted green
olives
¼ cup finely chopped mixed fresh herbs,
such as basil, marjoram, mint, oregano,
and parsley
salt and freshly ground black pepper

This recipe combines caponata, a popular relish in Italian restaurants, with Italian arborio rice, a risotto rice. The rice makes the salad extra special because it is from the Piedmont, along the valley of the Po River, one of Italy's most important rice-growing regions. If you have difficulty locating arborio rice, long-grain white rice may be substituted.

❖

❖ Bring 10 cups of water to a boil in a large saucepan. Stir in the salt. Add the rice and cook, uncovered, over a moderate heat for about 12 minutes, until *al dente*. Drain, rinse with cold water, and drain again. Set aside.

❖ While the rice is cooking, sauté the onion with 2 tbsp. of the oil in a large skillet over a moderately high heat. Cook for about 5 minutes, until the onion becomes translucent. Add the eggplant, garlic, and another tablespoon of the oil, and cook for about 7 minutes, until the eggplant is soft.

❖ Transfer the rice to a large bowl and toss with the remaining 3 tbsp. olive oil and the balsamic vinegar. Add the cooked eggplant mixture, tomatoes, capers, olives, and fresh herbs, tossing to mix well. Season with salt and pepper to taste. Let stand for at least 20 minutes before serving.

Lucky Black-eyed Pea Salad

Serves 8

INGREDIENTS
2 cups large macaroni
4 cups canned, black-eyed peas, drained
1 medium red bell pepper, chopped
1 medium green bell pepper, chopped
1 medium purple onion, chopped
6 oz. sliced provolone cheese, cut into strips
3 oz. sliced pepperoni, cut into strips
1 2-oz. jar diced pimento, drained
1 4½-oz. jar sliced mushrooms, drained
2 tbsp. chopped fresh parsley

DRESSING
1 0.7-oz. package Italian salad dressing mix, or of a mixture of 2 tsp. onion powder, 2 tsp. garlic salt, 2 tsp. ground oregano, ½ tsp. ground thyme, and ½ tsp. sweet, mild paprika
¼ tsp. pepper
¼ cup sugar
½ cup white wine vinegar
¼ cup canola oil

Black-eyed peas are not really peas, but beans. This salad is based on a Southern dish, a region where eating black-eyed peas is considered good luck. You can buy them at most markets selling Caribbean produce.

———— ❖ ————

❖ Cook the macaroni according to manufacturers' instructions. Drain well, and transfer to a large serving bowl. Set aside. Combine black-eyed peas, macaroni, bell peppers, onion, cheese, pepperoni, pimento, mushrooms, and parsley in a large bowl. Mix well and set aside.

❖ Place all the dressing ingredients in a jar with a tightly fitting lid. Cover and shake until ingredients are combined. Pour the dressing over the salad, mix gently, cover, and refrigerate for at least 2 hours before serving.

Moroccan Couscous Salad

Serves 4

INGREDIENTS
4 medium tomatoes
2 cups couscous, cooked according to manufacturers' instructions, and cooled
¼ cup chopped fresh basil
2 tbsp. chopped fresh parsley
1 tbsp. grated Parmesan cheese
1 tbsp. sunflower seeds
2 tsp. balsamic vinegar

This aromatic salad is influenced by the cuisine of Morocco, where couscous is a staple food. These individual salads served in scooped-out, ripe tomatoes make a pretty party dish.

———— ❖ ————

❖ Cut off and discard the tops of the tomatoes; scoop out the flesh without breaking the tomato shells. Chop the tomato flesh and place it in a large bowl. Add couscous, basil, parsley, cheese, sunflower seeds, and vinegar, tossing to mix well. Spoon the mixture evenly into the tomato shells. Refrigerate for at least 1 hour, or overnight, before serving.

RIGHT *Lucky Black-eyed Pea Salad*

Section Six

FRUIT AND NUT SALADS

Fresh Fruit with Peach Glaze

Serves 4

INGREDIENTS

*1 cup fruit juice, such as peach,
pineapple-orange-guava, pineapple-
orange-banana, mandarin orange,
or raspberry
½ tbsp. lemon juice
1½ tbsp. sugar
¼ tsp. finely grated lemon peel
½ tbsp. cornstarch
1 cup cubed fresh pineapple
1 cup sliced bananas
¾ cup cubed cantaloupe
¾ cup cubed kiwi fruit
¾ cup sliced nectarines
mint leaves, to decorate*

This salad will bring summer indoors, even in the dead of winter.

❖

❖ Combine the fruit juice, lemon juice, sugar, lemon peel, and cornstarch in a medium-size saucepan. Stir over a medium-high heat for 5 minutes, or until the mixture comes to a boil. Reduce the heat to low and cook for 2 minutes more, or until slightly thickened. Remove from heat and let cool slightly; alternatively, refrigerate the glaze until thoroughly chilled.

❖ To serve, arrange the fruit in four dessert dishes. Spoon the glaze over the fruit, and decorate with mint leaves.

Hawaiian Macadamia Salad

Serves 4–6

INGREDIENTS

*1 ripe papaya, quartered lengthwise with
seeds reserved
1 ripe avocado, peeled, pitted, and cut into
bite-size pieces.
8 loosely packed cups, bite-size lettuce
¼ cup toasted macadamia nuts
(see page 112)*

DRESSING

*2 tbsp. papaya seeds, measured out from
the reserved seeds
¼ cup canola oil
1 tbsp. lemon juice
1½ tsp. Dijon-style mustard
1 tsp. grated, peeled fresh ginger*

This zesty salad is accented by peppery papaya seeds and sweet, rich macadamia nuts. It can be combined with broiled, shelled shrimp to make a delectable entrée.

❖

❖ Place the papaya in a covered ceramic or plastic bowl, or in a heavy-duty resealable plastic bag, and refrigerate to chill.

❖ Prepare the dressing. Place the papaya seeds in a food processor or blender. Add the canola oil, lemon juice, mustard, ginger, salt, and pepper. Process until the papaya seeds are the size of coarsely crushed black pepper. Set aside.

❖ Peel the avocado, remove the pit, and cut into bite-size pieces. Transfer to a large bowl and add the lettuce. Pour over the dressing and toss to mix and coat evenly. Arrange on serving plates, top with the papaya, and sprinkle with the toasted macadamia nuts. Serve immediately.

RIGHT *Fresh Fruit with Peach Glaze*

Orange and Watercress Salad in Citrus Dressing

Serves 4

INGREDIENTS
1 large bunch watercress
2 medium oranges, peeled, seeded,
sectioned, and sliced crosswise
⅓ cup sliced scallions

CITRUS DRESSING
1½ tbsp. fresh lemon juice
1 tbsp. orange juice
¼ tsp. crushed dried mint
2 tbsp. olive oil
¼ tsp. salt

This refreshing fruit salad has a Caribbean flair, but the ingredients are easily available.

❖

❖ Rinse the watercress well. Remove and discard large stems, dry the leaves on paper towels, and refrigerate until chilled. To serve, place the watercress in a bowl or on a plate. Add orange sections and scallions. In a small bowl, mix all the dressing ingredients together to combine. Pour the dressing over the salad and toss gently. Serve immediately.

Creamy Orange and Endive Salad

Serves 4

INGREDIENTS
2 large Belgian endives
1 seedless orange
½ cup cream
1 tbsp. mustard
salt and pepper

Inspired by a German recipe, this salad combines the sweetness of cream and oranges with the bite of endive, mustard, and pepper.

❖

❖ Remove the outer leaves of the endives, using only the white leaves. Cut the leaves in half lengthwise and arrange on a serving platter. Peel the orange, removing the white pith. Finely shred the peel and blanch for 5 minutes to eliminate any bitterness. Drain, pat dry with a paper towel, and set aside to cool.

❖ Mix the cream with the mustard, and season with salt and pepper to taste. Pour over the endive. Sprinkle the shredded orange peel on top. Slice the remaining orange flesh and use to garnish the salad.

LEFT *Orange and Watercress Salad in Citrus Dressing*

Heavenly Honeyed Nuts

Makes about 2 cups

INGREDIENTS

2 cups whole almonds, pecans, or dry-
roasted peanuts
2 tbsp. soy sauce
2 tbsp. honey
½ tsp. finely grated orange peel
½ tsp. garlic powder
½ tsp. ground ginger
2 tsp. almond or vegetable oil

These nuts add crunch to green salads and fruit salads. They can be placed in resealable plastic bags and frozen for future use up to 6 months.

❖ Preheat the oven to 350°F. Spread the nuts in a shallow pan and toast in the oven for 15 minutes, stirring once or twice. Let cool. Reduce the oven temperature to 250°F.

❖ In a small saucepan, blend the soy sauce with the honey. Stir in the orange peel, garlic powder, and ginger. Bring the mixture to à boil over a medium heat. Stir in the toasted nuts and toss to coat evenly. Boil, stirring constantly, for 5 minutes, or until all the liquid is absorbed. Add the oil and stir again.

❖ Place the nuts in a single layer, spaced out, on a baking sheet. Bake in the center of the oven for 15 minutes. Pour out onto oiled aluminum foil or onto another nonstick surface. Toss and separate the nuts every 5 minutes until they are cool. Store the cooled nuts in a resealable plastic bag.

Toasted Nuts and Seeds

INGREDIENTS

shelled nuts, any type

❖ Preheat the oven to 350°F. Spread nuts or seeds on a baking pan and bake for 6–15 minutes, until they smell toasted and are darker in color. Stir once or twice while toasting to ensure even browning.

RIGHT *An assortment of toasted nuts and seeds*

Party Antipasto

Serves 4–6

INGREDIENTS
*1 head romaine lettuce, rinsed and dried
assorted cheeses, such as caraway, hot
pepper, and Monterey Jack, cut in wedges
melon wedges
2 cups fresh strawberries, rinsed and
hulled
1 cup fresh or canned pineapple chunks
2 cups seedless grapes, rinsed
2 cups Heavenly Honeyed Nuts, using
pecans (see page 112)*

Here is a colorful party tray filled with fruits, cheeses, and nuts. You can adapt the selection by choosing cheeses that are local specialties in your area. Most cheeses will go beautifully with honeyed pecans. Add some prosciutto or pancetta, crackers and condiments, and some fruity chilled wine to make your party menu complete.

——————— ❖ ———————

❖ Arrange lettuce leaves on a serving tray or platter. In layered rows, arrange cheese, melon, strawberries, pineapple, and grapes. Place honeyed nuts around the outside perimeters of the cheese, or place them in a bowl in the center of the platter.

Champagne-poached Pears

Serves 6

INGREDIENTS
*6 large unripe pears
6 cups dry champagne
1 cup sugar
1 3-inch cinnamon stick
8–20 juniper berries
1 dried red chile (optional)*

A dry white or sparkling wine may be substituted for the champagne in this adaptation of a South American dish.

——————— ❖ ———————

❖ Using a vegetable peeler, remove the skin from each pear, leaving the stem attached. Put the champagne, sugar, cinnamon, juniper berries, and the chile, if desired, into an enameled or stainless-steel pot. Place the pears in the pot. Bring to a boil, then lower the heat, and gently simmer for about 35 minutes, or until the pears are tender. With a wooden spoon, transfer the pears to a serving bowl. Continue to cook the poaching liquid over a medium heat for about 25 minutes, until the liquid has reduced to 2–2½ cups. Pour the hot syrup over the pears in the bowl, along with the cinnamon and a few of the juniper berries. Chill for 2 hours and serve.

RIGHT *Party Antipasto*

Cranberry Salad

Serves 4

INGREDIENTS

*1 cup fresh cranberries, finely ground in
food processor*
1½ cups miniature marshmallows
¼ cup granulated sugar
*1 cup diced, unpeeled tart apples, such as
Granny Smith or pippin apples*
¼ cup halved seedless grapes
¼ cup chopped pecans
½ cup heavy cream, whipped

I always think of Thanksgiving when it comes to cranberries, but this fruit salad can be served any time of the year. The salad would look especially pretty at Christmas in a wreath-shaped mold and garnished with fresh mint leaves.

—————— ❖ ——————

❖ Place the cranberries in a food processor or blender and process. In a large mixing bowl, combine the cranberries, marshmallows, and sugar. Refrigerate overnight. The next day, add the apples, grapes, and pecans to the bowl and mix well. Fold in the whipped cream and serve immediately.

Costa del Sol Cooler

Serves 4

INGREDIENTS

1½ cups tomato juice
1 ¼-oz. envelope unflavored gelatin
1 tbsp. cider vinegar
1 tbsp. lemon juice
⅛ tsp. garlic powder
¾ tsp. salt
⅛ tsp. black pepper
⅛ tsp. hot pepper sauce
1½ cups peeled and diced tomatoes
½ cup finely chopped cucumber
¼ cup finely chopped green bell pepper
⅛ cup finely chopped onion
⅛ cup finely chopped celery
⅓ cup dairy sour cream
*⅓ cup prepared mayonnaise, or
Homemade Mayonnaise (see page 29)*

Here's a refreshing, molded, gazapacho-style dish influenced by the famous cold soup of Costa del Sol in Spain. Use a light or non-fat prepared mayonnaise if you wish to cut down on calories and dairy fat.

—————— ❖ ——————

❖ Pour the tomato juice into a saucepan, and stir in the gelatin. Let stand for 2 minutes. Bring to a simmer over a medium-low heat, and stir until the gelatin has dissolved. Add the vinegar, lemon juice, garlic powder, salt, black pepper, and hot pepper sauce, and mix well. Transfer to a large bowl and refrigerate until the mixture has thickened slightly.

❖ Then add the tomatoes, cucumber, green bell pepper, onion, and celery to the tomato juice mixture. Pour into a lightly oiled 1½-quart ring mold and chill until firm. Meanwhile, combine the sour cream and mayonnaise, and chill.

❖ To serve, unmold the salad onto a large serving plate and mound a dollop of the sour cream mixture in the center.

LEFT *Cranberry Salad in the making*

Japanese Persimmon Salad

Serves 4

INGREDIENTS
4 tbsp. whole unblanched almonds
4 ripe persimmons
8 tsp. hazelnut or almond liqueur
bunch of small grapes or sliced fresh fig,
to garnish

This gorgeous deep-orange fruit is cultivated primarily in Japan and China, but persimmons are also grown in California, France, Spain, Italy, North Africa, and Chile.

❖ Preheat the oven to 325°F. Place the almonds in a baking pan and bake for 15 minutes, until lightly golden inside. Cool, then chop in coarse slivers.

❖ Gently cut out the leaf-stemmed end from each persimmon and discard. Halve each fruit lengthwise and place on a serving dish. With a sharp paring knife, deeply score a diamond pattern into the flesh, reaching almost to the skin. Drizzle the liqueur slowly over each persimmon half, squeezing the fruit gently to open the interstices. Sprinkle with the chopped almonds. Place several grapes or fig slices in the leaf cavity of each persimmon half, and serve.

Minty Melon Medley

Serves 4

INGREDIENTS
1 honeydew melon, cut into bite-size
chunks
1 cantaloupe, cut into bite-size chunks
1 pint blackberries, blueberries,
raspberries, or other in-season berries
1 10-oz. jar mint jelly
½ cup chopped fresh mint
¼ cup sugar
¼ cup water
mint sprigs, to decorate

This adaptation of a Pennsylvania-Dutch recipe makes excellent use of delicious summer fruits.

❖ Equally divide the melon chunks and berries between four bowls, and stir gently to mix. Cover and chill for at least 2 hours. Meanwhile, melt the mint jelly in the top of a double boiler. Stir in the chopped mint, sugar, and water. Transfer the mint mixture to a small bowl, cover, and refrigerate for about 1 hour, until well chilled. To serve, decorate the fruit salads with mint sprigs, and serve with the mint syrup.

RIGHT *Japanese Persimmon Salad*

Indian-style Carrot and Pine Nut Salad

Serves 4

INGREDIENTS

2 cups plain non-fat or low-fat yogurt
1 tbsp. packed brown sugar
¼ tsp. finely grated orange peel
2 tbsp. orange juice

¼ tsp. ground nutmeg or cardamom
salt
about 3 cups coarsely grated carrots
¼ cup raisins
3 tbsp. toasted pine nuts (see page 112)

Any favorite nuts, such as cashews, almonds, or pecans, can be substituted for the pine nuts in the recipe, but it is the pine nut that gives this dish its Indian flavor. Pine nuts, called *piñon*, are also used in cooking by Native Americans in Arizona and New Mexico.

❖

❖ In a medium-size bowl, stir together the yogurt, brown sugar, orange peel, orange juice, and nutmeg or cardamom. Add salt to taste. Fold in the carrots and raisins, sprinkle with the toasted pine nuts, and serve.

Drunken Banana Salad

Serves 4

INGREDIENTS

2 bananas, peeled and cut into rounds
2 oranges, peeled and sectioned
½ cup sweetened dried coconut

¼ cup brandy
¼ cup dark, Jamaican-style rum
1 tsp. sugar

Here is a sweet, lazy-day treat. With its luscious fruit and coconut, this salad will remind you of a tropical island.

❖

❖ Alternate slices of bananas, orange sections, and dried coconut in a fruit dish until full. Mix the brandy and rum with the sugar, pour over the salad, and serve.

LEFT *Indian-style Carrot and Pine Nut Salad*

Famous Waldorf Salad

Serves 4

INGREDIENTS
1¼ cups diced tart apples
1¼ cups seedless green grapes, or
2 8-oz. cans tropical fruit salad, drained
2 tbsp. shredded dried coconut (optional)
½ cup chopped pitted dates (optional)
⅓ cup diced celery
⅔ cup mayonnaise, plain yogurt, or
buttermilk
1 tbsp. walnut oil
2 tsp. fresh lemon or lime juice
1 tsp. sugar
¼ tsp. ground ginger
½ cup chopped walnuts

A simpler version of this salad was created by chef Oscar Tschirky in the 1890s for a party to celebrate the impending opening of the Waldorf-Astoria Hotel in New York. The recipe is included in this chapter because the salad really became popular when walnuts were added some years later. The tropical fruit and coconut are new additions, and give the salad a Caribbean touch.

❖

❖ In a large bowl, mix together the apples, grapes or tropical fruit, shredded coconut, dates, and celery. In a separate bowl, whisk together the mayonnaise, walnut oil, lemon or lime juice, sugar, and ginger. Pour the mixture over the salad and lightly toss. Cover and refrigerate. Just before serving, gently mix in the walnuts.

Turkish Cucumber Salad

Serves 4

INGREDIENTS
1 large cucumber, grated
1 cup yogurt
2 tbsp. blanched golden raisins
2 tbsp. chopped walnuts
1 small onion, finely chopped
salt and freshly ground black pepper
1 tsp. chopped fresh mint

The exotic mixture of cucumbers, raisins, nuts, and mint, all bound together with yogurt, makes this an exciting and tasty salad.

❖

❖ Place the cucumber, yogurt, raisins, walnut, and onion in a large bowl and stir to combine. Season with salt and pepper to taste. Blend in half the mint. Serve in the bowl or on four individual plates, with the remaining mint sprinkled on top to garnish.

LEFT *Waldorf Salad*

Easy Ambrosia Salad

Serves 4

INGREDIENTS

2 tbsp. plain low-fat yogurt or buttermilk
1 tbsp. maple syrup
½ pint strawberries, hulled and quartered
1 navel orange, peeled and chopped
2 kiwi fruit, peeled and chopped
¼ cup sweetened, flaked coconut

This extravagant version of ambrosia includes kiwi fruit and strawberries in addition to the classic ingredients of oranges and coconut.

❖ Gently mix the yogurt or buttermilk, maple syrup, strawberries, orange, kiwi fruit, and coconut together in a bowl, and serve.

Italian Orange and Red Onion Salad

Serves 4

INGREDIENTS

5 seedless oranges, peeled and sectioned
1 small red onion, sliced in rings
¼ cup olive oil
salt
1 tbsp. finely chopped fennel
1 tbsp. chopped fresh parsley

A favorite in the Italian countryside, this recipe makes a sweet and tangy salad. Be sure to use the sweetest and juiciest of oranges and the freshest ingredients.

❖ Toss the orange sections and onion rings with the olive oil in a bowl. Sprinkle with the fennel and parsley, and add salt to taste. Transfer to a large, resealable plastic bag and place in refrigerator for 1 hour; alternatively, leave in the bowl, cover, and baste at intervals with a little orange juice. Transfer the salad to a large serving plate or four individual plates to serve.

RIGHT *Easy Ambrosia Salad*

Nutty Spinach Salad

Serves 4

INGREDIENTS

1 bunch fresh spinach, rinsed and torn
into bite-size pieces
1½ cups sliced fresh mushrooms
¼ cup crumbled mild blue cheese
2 scallions, chopped
½ cup toasted hazelnuts (see page 112)
Classic French Vinaigrette (see page 22)
made with raspberry vinegar

This salad is popular in the Pacific Northwest region of the United States, around Portland, Oregon and Seattle, Washington, two major new gourmet centers of the nation.

———————— ❖ ————————

❖ Arrange the spinach on four salad plates. Top each plate with one-quarter of the mushrooms, then one-quarter each of the blue cheese, scallions, and toasted hazelnuts. Drizzle on a small amount of the raspberry vinaigrette, and pass the rest separately.

Peanut-Cilantro Melange

Serves 4

INGREDIENTS

½ cup plain non-fat or low-fat yogurt
¼ cup mayonnaise
1–1½ tsp. curry powder
1 tbsp. finely chopped fresh cilantro
salt and freshly ground black pepper
3 cups chopped cooked turkey or chicken
1 cup halved seedless green or purple
grapes
⅓ cup chopped water chestnuts
½ cup chopped green or red bell pepper
lettuce leaves
⅓ cup chopped dry-roasted peanuts

Originating in the Far East, this combination of tastes and textures is truly complex and exotic. You may like to substitute a low-fat or non-fat mayonnaise for the regular mayonnaise in the recipe to cut down on fats.

———————— ❖ ————————

❖ Place the yogurt, mayonnaise, curry powder, and cilantro in a large bowl and mix well to combine. Add salt and pepper to taste, and mix again. Fold in the turkey or chicken, the grapes, water chestnuts, and bell pepper. Cover and refrigerate to chill thoroughly. To serve, line four plates with lettuce leaves, top each with one-quarter of the salad and a sprinkling of the chopped peanuts.

LEFT *Nutty Spinach Salad*

Index